P9-EER-515

Jack Kerouac: "The Road Is Life"

Richard Worth
AR B.L.: 7.2
Points: 4.0   MG

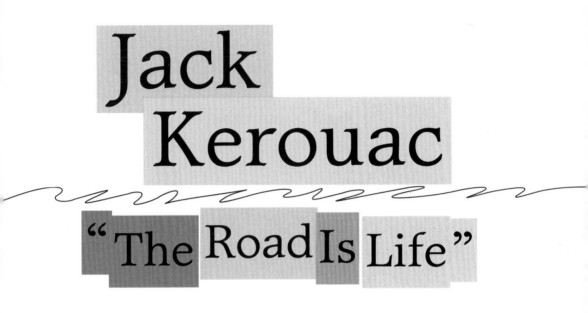

Jack Kerouac

"The Road Is Life"

Read about other
American REBELS

James Dean

*"Dream As If You'll
Live Forever"*

0-7660-2537-3

Kurt Cobain

*"Oh Well, Whatever,
Nevermind"*

0-7660-2426-1

Jimi Hendrix

"Kiss The Sky"

0-7660-2449-0

Madonna

"Express Yourself"

0-7660-2442-3

L T 31888

American REBELS

Jack Kerouac

"The Road Is Life"

Richard Worth

Enslow Publishers, Inc.
40 Industrial Road
Box 398
Berkeley Heights, NJ 07922
USA
http://www.enslow.com

Copyright © 2006 by Richard Worth

All rights reserved.

No part of this book may be reproduced by any means without the written permission of the publisher.

Library of Congress Cataloging-in-Publication Data

Worth, Richard.
     Jack Kerouac : "the road is life" / by Richard Worth.
         p. cm. — (American rebels)
     Includes bibliographical references and index.
     ISBN 0-7660-2448-2
     1. Kerouac, Jack, 1922–1969—Juvenile literature. 2. Authors, American—
20th century—Biography—Juvenile literature. I. Title. II. Series.
     PS3521.E735Z97 2006
     813'.54—dc22

                                        2005037884

Printed in the United States of America

10 9 8 7 6 5 4 3 2 1

To Our Readers: We have done our best to make sure all Internet Addresses in this book were active and appropriate when we went to press. However, the author and the publisher have no control over and assume no liability for the material available on those Internet sites or on other Web sites they may link to. Any comments or suggestions can be sent by e-mail to comments@enslow.com or to the address on the back cover.

Text Credits: Excerpts from *Memory Babe: A Critical Biography of Jack Kerouac* are © 1983 by Gerald Nicosia and are used with permission, quotes appear on pp. 20–21 (notes 12 and 13), 56–57 (notes 10 and 11), 58 (notes 13 and 14), 68, 72 (note 16), 73, 111 (note 2), 115 (note 10), 116, 117 (note 13); From *JACK'S BOOK* by Barry Gifford and Lawrence Lee, Copyright © 1994 by the authors and reprinted by permission of the St. Martin's Press, quotes appear on pp. 21 (note 14), 26 (note 2), 35, 43 (note 12), 66 (note 3), 126, 128, 129–131, 133; Reprinted by permission of SLL/Sterling Lord Literistic, Inc., Copyright by John Sampas, Literary Rep., quotes appear on pp. 27 (notes 4 and 5), 36 (note 12), 38, 44 (note 15), 45, 47 (note 17), 49 (note 20), 50, 51 (notes 2, 4, and 5), 54, 63 (note 24), 66 (note 2), 67 (note 6), 74 (note 20), 78, 81, 97 (note 21), 110, 112 (note 4), 115 (note 11), 117–118 (notes 14 and 15), 119, 122 (note 22).

Illustration Credits: Allen Ginsberg/CORBIS, pp. 34, 46, 59, 69; Associated Press/AP, pp. 8, 76, 86, 120, 132; © Corel Corporation, p. 79; © 2006 Jupiterimages Corporation, pp. 23, 103, 123; Library of Congress, p. 16; Wikipedia.com, p. 107.

Cover Illustration: Associated Press/AP.

Contents

Chapter 1

Fame

Suddenly Jack Kerouac was famous. He had dreamed of this moment during most of his career as a writer. In 1957, Viking Publishers released his novel, *On the Road*. The novel fictionalized Kerouac's own travels across America. *On the Road* also popularized a group of novelists and poets called the Beat Generation. They had rebelled against middle-class life. Like Kerouac, the rest of the beats did not want nine-to-five jobs. They managed to live on little or no money in cities like New York or San Francisco. Their lifestyle appealed to many young Americans. As author Bruce Cook put it:

> With the publication of *On the Road*, there was a sort of instantaneous flash of recognition that seemed to send thousands of them [young Americans] into the streets, proclaiming that Kerouac had written their story, that *On the Road* was their book. There was such community of

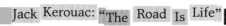

Jack Kerouac, 1962

feeling in this response that critics began to speak
with some certainty . . . of Kerouac's as the new
literary generation.[1]

Jack Kerouac was changing America.

The reviews for *On the Road* were generally good.
One reviewer said that it was "the most beautifully
executed, the clearest, and the most important utterance
yet made by the generation Kerouac himself named years
ago as 'beat' . . ."[2] Articles about the Beat Generation
began appearing on the newsstands in popular
magazines such as *Harper's Bazaar* and *Mademoiselle*.
Other stories were published in newspapers such as
The New York Times.

The novel appeared while America was still idolizing
a young actor named James Dean. Dean had appeared
in only a few films before his tragic death in a car
accident in 1955. However, he had become a hero to
many American young people. In his life and film roles,
Dean was a rebellious youth who did not live by the
traditional values of society. Some young people even
tried to look and dress like Dean.

At the same time, others were trying to look like
a rock-and-roll star named Elvis Presley. During the
1950s, Presley had rocketed to stardom with a new
musical sound and an electric style of performance.
As Presley sang, played his guitar, and wiggled his hips
on stage, many young people yelled and screamed with
delight over the young singer. He rapidly became a
teenage idol. The Beat Generation of writers, like Jack
Kerouac, seemed to exemplify the changes that were

occurring in America. Young people were looking for new heroes, like Dean, Presley, and Kerouac.

On the Road appeared on best-seller lists across America. Kerouac went on television where he was interviewed in front of an audience that numbered an estimated 40 million viewers. More interviews followed, and book parties were given by his publishers to promote his new book. Jack Kerouac had become one of the most important writers of his generation.

For the author of *On the Road*, however, life had begun quite differently.

Chapter 2

Early Life in Lowell

Jean-Louis (Jack) Kerouac was born on March 12, 1922, in Lowell, Massachusetts. Jack's parents, Leo and Gabrielle, were French Canadian. The Kerouac family had originally lived in Brittany, located in western France. During the early eighteenth century, however, Francois-Joachim Le Bihan de Kerouac (who spelled his name *Kervoac*) had emigrated to New France, which later became part of Canada. For over one hundred years, French settlers had lived in Canada. They established important towns at Montreal and Quebec along the St. Lawrence River.

In Canada, the Kerouacs became fur traders, known as *coureur de bois*, as well as farmers. In the late nineteenth century, Jack's grandfather, Jean-Baptiste, left Canada and moved to Nashua, New Hampshire. Jean-Baptiste and his wife, Clementine, had fifteen children. One of them was Leo Kerouac, Jack's father. Leo was born in 1889. After attending school in

Nashua, Leo became a printer. At first he worked for the *Nashua Telegraph*, the most important newspaper in town. His work there impressed the newspaper's owner. He also owned a French-Canadian newspaper in Lowell, Massachusetts. Leo Kerouac was transferred there and put in charge of the newspaper, *L'Etoile* (*The Star*).

By the mid-nineteenth century, Lowell had become the center of the Industrial Revolution in the United States. Cotton, imported from Southern plantations, was brought to Lowell and turned into cotton cloth. By 1850, Lowell had forty mills, ten thousand looms, and more than ten thousand mill workers. Some of them were French Canadians. The mills were often six stories high and lined the Merrimack River. Water from the river powered waterwheels that in turn drove the looms. As one European visitor put it, "Niagara [Falls] and Lowell are the two objects I will longest remember in my American journey, the one the glory of American scenery, the other of American industry."[1]

By 1850, Lowell had forty mills, ten thousand looms, and more than ten thousand mill workers.

Lowell continued to be a major manufacturing community into the early twentieth century, when Leo Kerouac arrived there. While working in Lowell during the week, he returned to Nashua on the weekends where he was dating Gabrielle Levesque. Born in 1895, Gabrielle had grown up in Nashua and worked in a shoe factory. Gabrielle and Leo Kerouac were married in 1915. They moved to Lowell and had three children. Gerard was born in 1916, Caroline in 1918, and Jack in 1922.

Childhood in Lowell

When Jack was a child, English was barely spoken in the Kerouac household. Instead, both parents and children spoke Joual. This was a French dialect used by the French Canadians who lived along parts of the St. Lawrence River. English was Jack's second language, which he learned in school. "All my knowledge," he later said, "rests in my 'French Canadianness' and nowhere else. The English language is a tool lately found. . . . I refashion it to fit French images."[2]

Lowell had a variety of immigrant groups who had come to work in the mills. They included French, Greeks, and Portuguese. Many of them were devoutly Roman Catholic. Jack was baptized as an infant in the Roman Catholic Church. His mother prayed regularly, holding rosary beads in her hands. Among the pictures in the Kerouac home was one of Saint Thérèse de Lisieux, a Catholic saint widely revered by many French Canadians. As a nun, she performed numerous miracles, according to the Church. One Catholic pope, Pius XI, called her "the greatest saint of modern times."

Gabrielle Kerouac directed many of her prayers to Saint Thérèse, hoping to save the life of her oldest son, Gerard. He suffered from a disease called rheumatic fever. This disease is caused by a bacterial infection. It eventually results in a weakening of the tissues of the heart, brain, and other organs. As Tom Clark, one of Jack Kerouac's biographers, has written, Jack "looked up to his invalid brother with a reverence that bordered on adoration and so believed implicitly in the remarkable sanctity of Gerard."[3]

Years later, Kerouac wrote about his brother in a book titled *Visions of Gerard*. He described his older brother taking him on walks in the woods. He wrote that Gerard was extremely kind to animals. Once he found a mouse in a trap and rescued it. Gerard took the mouse home, fed the animal, and built a little house for it in a basket. Gerard also enjoyed playing with an Erector toy set that his parents had bought for him. He often built "ferris wheels and race cars . . . and trucks that were borrowed from the book of instructions—Heaving the book aside he'd of a sick morning (as I watch) whip up beautiful little baby carriages or baby cribs for Nin (Caroline) to put her dolls in at noon. . . ."[4]

Gerard often played in bed because he was too sick to attend the Catholic school where his parents sent him. Once when he had gone to class, Gerard fell asleep. When awakened by one of the nuns, Gerard said that he had dreamed about going to heaven. This only increased his aura of saintliness in the eyes of his younger brother, Jack. Indeed, Jack was convinced that he could never be as good a person as Gerard.

Jack later wrote that Gerard "left me his heart but not his tender countenance and sorrowful patience and kindly lights. . . ."[5]

During 1926, Gerard continued to grow sicker and sicker. Jack could hear him at night when Gerard could not sleep because of the pain caused by his disease. "Lancing pain in the legs and vague pain in the chest wakes Gerard in the mid of night, he makes a soft groan and represses even that realizing we're all asleep. . . ."[6] Eventually, Gerard died on June 2. As Kerouac put it, "Death is the other side of the same coin, we call now, Life."[7] Gerard's death seemed to confirm the Kerouac family motto, "Aimer, Travailler, Souffrir," meaning "Love, Work, and Suffer."

> Jack "looked up to his invalid brother with a reverence that bordered on adoration . . ."

According to Kerouac, he and his brother had a little disagreement before Gerard's death. Jack had knocked over one of Gerard's structures built with the Erector set. Gerard had slapped Jack for it. Gerard later apologized. But Jack was still angry at him. Like other small children, Jack felt that he somehow possessed unusual powers. Just by being angry at someone, Jack believed that he could make evil befall the person. Therefore, he felt guilty because he thought he had caused Gerard's death. This guilt remained with Jack for a lifetime.[8]

Kerouac grew up in Lowell, Massachusetts, a working-class town.

Going to School

The Kerouacs moved to a new home a year later, hoping to put the death of Gerard behind them. By this time, Leo Kerouac had his own successful printing business. He published a small newspaper describing the movies and live performances that appeared at local theaters in Lowell. Ti Jean, or Small Jean, as Jack was called at home, was sent to Saint Louis de France. This was a local Catholic school. The school was located in Centralville, a French-Canadian section of Lowell, where the Kerouac family lived. When he was not attending school, Jack went with his father downtown to the print shop. Among the Irish immigrants who worked in the shop, Jack began to learn some English.

Jack also developed a very close relationship with his mother. In the past, Jack feared that his mother loved Gerard more than she loved him.[9] But this changed after Gerard's death. Sometimes at night, when Jack was afraid of the dark, he would climb into bed with his mother. By 1933, Gabrielle Kerouac had transferred Jack to another Catholic school, Saint Joseph's. Here he was required to "learn to read, speak, and write in English." According to Paul Maher, one of Kerouac's biographers, Jack "quickly mastered the intricacies of English, so much so that it became his primary language for the rest of his life."[10]

Meanwhile, Jack was already beginning to do some writing on his own. His father regularly went to a nearby racetrack, and sometimes Jack accompanied him. Jack developed a make-believe game of horse racing and wrote a small newspaper about racing called *Turf*. He later developed another newspaper called *Baseball Chatter*. Jack was fascinated by the sport and followed major-league baseball closely each season. At age eleven, Jack wrote a short novel based on *The Adventures of Huckleberry Finn*, written by one of his favorite authors, Mark Twain. Jack also kept a journal where he recorded the weather and some of the games that he played with friends. Gerard had been a cartoonist, who had taught Jack how to draw. He wrote and illustrated his own small comic books. They were based on popular magazine characters, like the detective known as "The Shadow."

The Great Depression

While Jack was still in elementary school, America was struck by the Great Depression. Following the stock market crash of 1929, economic conditions grew worse until an estimated 25 percent of adult workers were unemployed. Many people in Lowell were thrown out of work at the mills. For a while, Leo Kerouac continued to run his print shop, producing programs for the local theaters as well as other materials. As a result, Jack often received free tickets to the movies where he watched Westerns and other films. These gave him ideas for his own writing. A quiet teenager, Jack spent much of his time reading in the local library or writing.

By the mid-1930s, however, Leo Kerouac's business

had also declined. He earned extra money running the bowling alley at a local social club. Sometimes Jack visited his father and shot pool at the club. Then in March 1936, the Merrimack River flooded. Many homes and businesses, including his father's print shop, were flooded out by the high water. The family was forced to move to a cheaper home. Leo Kerouac took a job with the Works Progress Administration (WPA). This was a program set up by President Franklin Roosevelt during the 1930s to provide jobs for men thrown out of work as a result of the Depression. The WPA cleared land to create new parks, built recreation centers, and handled other projects. Gabrielle Kerouac took a job at a local

> **Sometimes Jack visited his father and shot pool at the club.**

shoe factory. She earned extra money to buy food and help pay the rent on the Kerouacs' home. Nevertheless, the family was forced to leave their home for another, cheaper apartment.

Moving from home to home was a regular part of Jack Kerouac's childhood. As Paul Maher wrote: "The constant uprooting of the two surviving Kerouac children (Jack and his sister) from their friends implanted an early sense of the rootlessness that would plague them in later years."[11]

Success in High School

By 1936, Jack was enrolled at Lowell High School. He had not lost his interest in writing and hoped to become a professional journalist. He read books by well-known novelists, such as Jack London. London was the author of *White Fang* and other novels about the Alaskan wilderness. These influenced Jack's own writing. Jack confided his goals to a local priest, Father Armand Morissette. Jack explained that most people in Lowell laughed when he told them of his plans. "I'm not laughing," Father Morissette told him. "But it's a rough life, you know." Jack said that his friends warned him that he should "work like everybody else! Don't be a bum!" But the priest recognized that Jack had a legitimate ambition to be a writer. "You're from a poor family," Father Morissette cautioned him, "you'll have to try for a scholarship."[12]

> **"You're from a poor family," Father Morissette cautioned him, "you'll have to try for a scholarship."**

Fortunately, Jack had been sharpening his abilities as an athlete when he wasn't reading or writing. Jack played baseball for a team called the Pawtucket Blues, named after a section of Lowell. He was a good hitter and outfielder. But as biographer Gerald Nicosia wrote, football was the sport at which he really excelled.

> He developed a rugged style of blocking by butting his opponents in the stomach, thirty years before headfirst tackles came into fashion in professional football. For years he had been improving his speed as a track runner. . . .Though he was only about five feet eight, he had big thighs that drove his legs like pistons, and he had been building his body with an

Olympic exercise program. . . .Once he got around
the end with a football, few could catch him.[13]

Jack began to build a reputation for himself on the
football team at Lowell High School. Nevertheless, he
still had a hard time convincing Coach Tom Keady to
start him in every game. Jack did not always follow
the instructions that Coach Keady gave him. However,
on Thanksgiving Day 1938, Jack distinguished himself
in a game against Lawrence, Massachusetts. In front
of fourteen thousand fans, Jack scored the winning
touchdown on a pass from the quarterback. According
to his boyhood friend Scotty Beaulieu, "Jack was hard
as a rock, a great athlete. When I tackled him, or tried
to, once, when I grabbed his legs—man, I saw stars!
He plowed right through me."[14]

Attending the game were scouts from Boston College
as well as from Columbia University in New York City.
Both schools were interested in giving Jack a scholarship
if he played football. Jack's mother wanted him to
choose Columbia. She had great faith in Jack's ability
to become successful as a writer. She believed that New
York City was the best place for him to expose himself
to a variety of ideas that would shape his writing. Jack
was also interested in New York. "I wanted to dig New
York and become a big journalist in the big city beat,"
he said.[15]

His father, on the other hand, wanted Jack to
attend Boston College. He had taken a job at a printing
company that did a lot of work for Boston College.

Meanwhile, Jack had fallen in love with a young woman named Mary Carney, who did not want him to leave Lowell. She hoped to marry Jack, settle down in town, and raise a family.

However, Jack had decided that he needed to leave Lowell in order to pursue a writing career. He finally selected Columbia. Nevertheless, Jack was not permitted to attend Columbia in September 1939. He had not completed enough credits in mathematics and language arts.[16] Instead, he was required to attend Horace Mann, an exclusive preparatory school in the Bronx, New York. Given a scholarship, Jack found himself in the company of boys whose families were among the wealthiest in the United States. Jack continued writing at the prep school and read some of the stories of Ernest Hemingway. He was a famous novelist who had begun writing during the 1920s. Jack's short story, called "The Brothers," which shows a little Hemingway influence, was published in the prep school magazine. It was Jack's first published work.

> **Jack's short story, called "The Brothers" was published in the prep school magazine.**

Jack also listened to jazz in New York. Although his interest in jazz had begun in Lowell, it increased as he attended musical performances in New York. As he wrote in an article for the Horace Mann magazine, jazz was "music which has not been prearranged—free-for-all

Jack Kerouac's love of jazz music, with its "soulful expression and super-improvisation," influenced his writing style.

ad-lib. It is the outburst of passionate musicians, who pour all their energy into their instruments in the quest of soulful expression and super-improvisation."[17]

Jack would use the same approach in his own writing in the years ahead. His move to the cultural center of New York City provided just the environment he needed to pursue his writing.

Chapter 3

A Writer in New York

In September 1940, Jack Kerouac entered Columbia University. He spent much of his time at lengthy football practices, directed by the university coach Lou Little. No matter how hard Kerouac practiced, Coach Little did not seem to think he was good enough to be a starter on the team. When he was not practicing, Kerouac studied and wrote term papers for some of his classmates. This helped him earn extra money for college expenses. When he finally did play in an early game against Columbia rival Rutgers—located in New Jersey—Kerouac fractured a bone in his leg and was laid up with a cast.

With free time away from football practices, Kerouac now had more time to read. Among his favorite authors was Thomas Wolfe. Born in Ashville, North Carolina, in 1900, Wolfe later moved to Brooklyn, New York, and published his first novel in 1929. *Look Homeward,*

Angel, with its rich prose and use of numerous adjectives, appealed to Kerouac. As Wolfe put it, "Everything I write is immensely flavored with me."[1] Wolfe's novel was based on his own experiences—his travels, his observations of people, his own suffering, and his growing up in America. In 1935, Wolfe also published another novel, *Of Time and the River*, which described portions of his life not covered in *Look Homeward, Angel*. Other novels by Wolfe were published following his death from tuberculosis—a lung disease—in 1938. Kerouac based much of his work on his own experiences, much the way Wolfe had done.

When he was not reading Wolfe, Kerouac found himself cutting classes at college to experience life in New York City. He went to jazz clubs and met people, as he imagined Wolfe had done when he lived in New York. Kerouac also stayed in touch with some of the people whom he had known in Lowell. Scotty Beaulieu came to visit him in New York. "I went to visit Zagg [Jack's nickname] in New York City. He showed us around Columbia University."[2] Kerouac also went back to Lowell and visited with Sebastian Sampas. He was attending Emerson College in Boston. The two had gone to high school together, and Jack had often visited Sampas at his home. There he found books by the Irish novelist James Joyce who wrote *Portrait of the Artist as a Young Man*. In this novel, Joyce based the main character's life on his experiences in Dublin, Ireland.

There he discovered his calling to become a writer. As Kerouac told Sampas during one of their visits in the early 1940s, "I wanta be a writer."[3]

Life Outside Columbia

During the summer of 1941, Kerouac's parents moved to West Haven, Connecticut. "We look smack at the sea," he recalled. "Our street is filled with summer resort people—it is a summer resort, but a few people on the street live here the year 'round. To our right is a beach. Rowboats, skiffs, sailboats, and the like dot the shimmering tide. . . .The cottage has five rooms. . . . Ma's bed faces the sea."[4] Leo Kerouac had found a new job with a local printer.

Although Jack Kerouac returned to Columbia, he was growing tired of football practice. With the season barely underway, Kerouac decided to walk out on the football team and the university. He boarded a bus and headed for Washington, D.C. He was leaving the conventional lifestyle of college. As he wrote to Sampas, "I don't know what I've done—afraid to go home, too proud and too sick to go back to the football team, driven and weary with no place to go, I know not a soul."[5]

Jack Kerouac had carried out his first rebellion. As he later wrote in a poem: "At 18, I suddenly discovered/ the delight of rebellion . . . It/ruined my first College year./But after the drunken stage,/I shortly gathered up my reins/and began to direct those daring/white steeds of rebellion into/a more constructive direction. . . ."[6]

Kerouac eventually headed north and returned to his

parents' home in West Haven, Connecticut. His father was very upset that his son had given up a scholarship to college. Jack Kerouac found a job at a nearby factory, but lasted only one day at the work. To him, it seemed to be such a waste of time. He left North Haven and traveled to nearby Hartford, Connecticut. There he went to work at a local gas station.

While Kerouac worked in Hartford in 1941, he continued to write stories. A collection of his short stories, which included some of those written in Hartford, was later published in a book titled *Atop an Underwood*. Kerouac wrote his stories on an old Underwood typewriter. They included "Hartford after Work" and "Woman Going to Hartford." The stories and poems contained people whom Kerouac had met while he was working in Hartford as well as his own thoughts about being a writer.

World War II had been raging in Europe since 1939. Germany had conquered most of Western Europe, except England, which continued to stand its ground. However, many Americans were reluctant to get involved in the conflict until the United States was directly attacked. By late 1941, Kerouac had left Hartford. His parents had returned to Lowell, and he moved back in with them. In December, Kerouac and his parents heard the news that the Japanese had attacked the American naval base at Pearl Harbor, Hawaii. The United States declared war on Japan as well as its allies, Germany and Italy.

Atop an Underwood

Jack Kerouac's early work was collected and published in
1999, thirty years after his death. In one of the stories,
"Where the Road Begins," Kerouac described leaving home
for the first time, as he did when he went to New York:

> You sit in the train, and you begin to feel yourself
> eased away, away, away . . . . . and the gray home
> town is left behind, the prosaic existence of 18 years is
> now being discarded into the receptacle of Time . . . . .
> You see the old familiar things: streets with time-worn
> names, houses with barren roofs and upthrusting
> chimneys, staring tiredly at the same old sky, the same
> old heavens, the same old ashen emptiness. You look
> at all this and you tingle. You can feel a shudder of
> expectancy course through your tense, vibrant body.
> Your eyes swell with what you think is joy. You
> envision the Big City—and you squirm in your seat
> happily.

In another story, titled "New York Nite Club," Kerouac
described the night life in a bar:

> Outside, in the street, the sudden music which comes
> from the nitespot fills you with yearning for some
> intangible joy—and you feel that it can only be found
> within the smoky confines of the place. You leave the
> street and enter New York's night life. . . .There is
> the eternal smoke of cigarettes, the fine smell of bars
> ranged with colorful displays of bottles, gowned
> women, tuxedoed men, and those who reminisce,
> wrangle, and cry at the bar. . . .The music will soon
> begin—the little [black] trumpeter is almost ready, but
> never quite begins.[7]

Kerouac and World War II

Shortly after Pearl Harbor, Kerouac applied to the U.S. Navy to become part of their flight program. Meanwhile, he took a position at the *Lowell Sun* newspaper as a sports reporter. But this job lasted only a few months before Kerouac became bored with it. Since he had heard nothing from the Navy, Kerouac decided to leave Lowell. He went back on the road again as he had a year earlier. He headed back to Washington, D.C., hoping to meet more people and have more experiences for his book. On his travels, Kerouac met George Murray, a member of the merchant marine.

Kerouac became a sailor aboard the U.S.S. *Dorchester*, headed for Greenland.

In 1942, the U.S. Merchant Marine was transporting supplies to Great Britain and the Soviet Union, another ally of the United States. Merchant marine ships were also taking construction workers to locations like Greenland to build new military bases. As they sailed across the North Atlantic, these ships were protected by U.S. naval vessels. The North Atlantic was infested with German submarines, and many transport ships were sunk by torpedoes.

Nevertheless, Kerouac was excited about the idea of joining the merchant marine. After talking with Murray, Kerouac became a sailor aboard the U.S.S. *Dorchester*, headed for Greenland. As the ship sailed northward along the rough Atlantic seas, Kerouac regarded this adventure as another opportunity to gain experiences for his writing.[8] For the first time, Kerouac saw icebergs in the cold North Atlantic. He climbed a mountain on Greenland, saw local people called Inuit, and his ship barely escaped a submarine attack on the return voyage to the United States.

By the time the U.S.S. *Dorchester* docked in New York Harbor, Kerouac had experienced enough life at sea. In fall 1942, he was asked to come back to Columbia and play on the football team again. Soon after his return, however, Kerouac realized that nothing had changed. Coach Little still did not intend to make Kerouac a starter in any of the games. Football practice bored him. However, Kerouac did receive praise from Columbia's professors for the writing he produced in their English classes.

Nevertheless, this was not enough to keep him in college. He dropped out once again—leaving college life. Kerouac moved in with Edith (Edie) Parker. Parker was a wealthy young woman from Michigan, whom Kerouac had met in 1941. She was attending art classes. But after a short time living with her, Kerouac grew restless again. He enlisted in the U.S. Navy so he could serve in World War II. Kerouac went to Newport, Rhode Island, for basic training in 1943.

Navy life was very difficult for Kerouac to endure. He resented the regulations that required him to go to bed and get up at a specific time each day. Kerouac also resented taking orders from his superiors. They ordered him to spend long hours marching, cleaning the barracks, and wearing a navy uniform. He finally refused to put up with the discipline any longer. His superiors believed that Kerouac was suffering from psychological problems. Navy guards took him off to a military hospital, where he was examined by psychiatrists. They eventually decided that Kerouac was not suited for military life. Because of emotional problems, he was given a medical discharge in 1943.

While Kerouac was struggling with the military, his friend Sebastian Sampas had enlisted in the U.S. Army. In January 1944, Sampas participated in the American invasion of Anzio, Italy. During the battle against enemy forces, Sampas was wounded and died in March. It was a heavy blow to Kerouac, much like losing his brother, Gerard, many years earlier.

Life in New York City

During much of 1944, Kerouac bounced around from one place to another. This restlessness would continue during his entire adult life. Part of the time Kerouac spent with his parents. They had moved from Lowell to a new home in Ozone Park, Queens, outside of New York City. His father had found another job at a printing shop, while his mother worked at a shoe factory. Kerouac shipped out briefly with the merchant marine on a voyage to England. After his return to New York in the fall, he moved in again with Edie Parker.

In Parker's apartment, Kerouac became part of a

new circle of friends. Among them was Allen Ginsberg, a student at Columbia University. Ginsberg was impressed with the amount of writing that Kerouac had already done. One of Ginsberg's friends was Lucien Carr, son of a wealthy family from St. Louis, Missouri. Another member of Kerouac's circle was William S. Burroughs—a Harvard University graduate and a friend of Lucien Carr's.

When Kerouac met Carr, he was involved in a conflict with an old acquaintance from St. Louis, named David Kammerer. Kammerer was older than Carr and relentlessly stalked him. One evening, after having a few drinks with Carr at a bar, Kerouac met Kammerer on the street. Kammerer was looking for Carr. Kerouac told Kammerer where to find Carr, and Kammerer left. Later Carr met Kammerer and murdered him, stabbing Kammerer repeatedly with a knife. After disposing of the body, Carr asked Kerouac to help him hide the weapon. Carr eventually turned himself in to the police. He was convicted of manslaughter and sentenced to twenty years in prison. However, he was released after only two years. Kerouac was interrogated by local detectives. Kerouac remained in jail for over a week. Although the police believed that he was not involved in the murder, they were holding him as a witness. Kerouac contacted his father, asking him to put up bail money for his release. But his father was very angry with Jack and refused. Eventually, Edie Parker

Kerouac remained in jail for over a week.

Kerouac poses with a few of his writer friends near the Columbia University campus in 1944 or 1945. From left to right are: Hal Chase, Jack Kerouac, Allen Ginsberg, and William S. Burroughs.

agreed to put up bail for Kerouac. In return, he agreed to marry her.[9] The couple was married on August 22, 1944, while Kerouac was still in jail. Soon afterward, they went to Michigan where they lived with her wealthy family.

Jazz and Drugs

After only a few weeks, Kerouac had again grown restless. Marriage to Edie Parker was far too restricting for Kerouac. He also seemed poorly suited for a long-term relationship. As one of his friends, the poet Gary Snyder, put it, "Jack didn't live in a way that a reliable relationship could be established. . . . Jack was not about to order his life in such a way that he could be responsible to another person. And he never did demonstrate any interest in doing that."[10]

Kerouac left Michigan, while still married to Parker, and shipped out on another merchant marine ship. When he returned to New York with very little money, he moved into the dormitory room of Allan Ginsberg on the Columbia campus. Kerouac continued to write. In fact, he estimated that since 1939, he had written almost five hundred thousand words.[11] Kerouac was also writing a novel with William S. Burroughs, based on the Kammerer murder. Indeed, Kerouac had persuaded Burroughs to try his hand at writing. While they were busy writing, Burroughs also introduced Jack to the drug scene in New York. Kerouac smoked marijuana and tried morphine, a powerful narcotic. He was also introduced to Benzedrine, an amphetamine.

These dangerous drugs stimulate users, giving them more energy to stay awake for long periods.

Meanwhile, Edie Parker had come back from Michigan. The couple moved in with one of Parker's friends, named Joan Adams. Both Kerouac and Parker soon realized that their marriage was not working, and by 1946 they had ended their relationship. "I've asked Edie for a divorce," Kerouac wrote his sister.

> I'll go on seeing her occasionally, for we are both wacky in a way, and we should never have gotten married but just gone on knowing each other in a casual sort of way. . . . The happiest days of my life, I can tell you, were spent living with her at Columbia when all the kids were around, including Lucien. . . . I don't know, but to me a home in the suburbs is a sort of isolated hell where nothing happens.[12]

Not only did Kerouac have to deal with the end of his marriage, he also faced his father's death. Leo Kerouac had developed stomach cancer.

One day, when Jack was visiting his father, they argued about "how to brew coffee. A little later," according to Kerouac biographer Tom Clark, "Leo hunched forward in his chair . . . it was death. Jack held his father in his arms for the last time, and as he did, noticed the printer's ink still staining Leo's fingers." He was deeply saddened by his father's death.[13]

Kerouac and his father had not gotten along with each other. Leo Kerouac believed that his son was making a mistake in his pursuit of a writer's life. No matter what his father had told him, Kerouac was still determined to become a published novelist. In New York, he continued gathering material for a novel and began writing. Part of this material came from nightclubs that Kerouac visited and where he listened to jazz. Kerouac hoped to work this material into a new novel that he was writing during 1946. Up to this point, Kerouac had regarded himself as a failure. He had been unable to publish anything, although he had sent short stories to several magazines.

Bebop

Jazz had originated in the South during the nineteenth century. It was based on African-American hymns and spiritual songs. Gradually, jazz moved from the South, up the Mississippi River to Chicago, Illinois, and on to New York City. During the 1940s, a new form of jazz, called bebop, was being played in New York. Musicians like Dizzy Gillespie and Charlie Parker played bebop in New York clubs, especially in Harlem. Instead of large jazz bands, which had been popular during the 1930s, smaller jazz groups played bebop. Music became more complex, as bebop musicians departed from familiar melodies and played more improvisation. They improvised by adding their own melodies to the original songs. Bebop was faster than traditional jazz. It attracted a new generation of jazz musicians, such as pianist Thelonious Monk and drummers like Max Roach and Kenny Clarke. Instead of listening or dancing, as they did to traditional jazz, people just listened to bebop. As critic John Andrews wrote: "For the first time serious listening to the music, especially the improvised solos, became primary."[14]

By finishing a novel and getting it published, Jack hoped to prove himself and achieve success as a novelist. He believed that publishing the novel he was currently writing would justify his choice of lifestyle. "When this book is finished, which is going to be the sum and substance . . . of everything I've been thru," he wrote, "I shall be redeemed."[15]

Chapter 4

First Novel

The Town and the City was Jack Kerouac's first novel.
According to critic Douglas Brinkley, "Kerouac was
driven to write [the novel] by the grief he experienced
at the death of his father, Leo. . . ."[1] The long book
tells the story of the Martin family living in Galloway,
located on the Merrimack River. The Martins are partly
based on Kerouac's own family and Galloway is Lowell,
Massachusetts.

As he wrote the book, Kerouac kept a diary of his
feelings as a writer. On one day in June 1947, he wrote:
"Feeling just as hopeless—feeling that I may not, after
all, be able to complete anything. But I wrote 2000-
words pertaining to the chapter, and things begin to
break, or crumble & seethe."[2] In his diary, Kerouac
kept a record of how many words he wrote each day.
Before Kerouac began to write, he would pray for divine
direction, hoping that God would guide his pen along
the page. He asked himself why he wrote, when it

was often so difficult. "Why do I do it? It's a form of brooding, I actually look like a *hound-dog* all day. And how my mother is used to it! I think if I were not around the house brooding she would be certain the wheels of the universe had stopped turning."[3]

Kerouac did most of his writing in Ozone Park, where his mother lived. But the early parts of the book are set in Galloway, that is, Lowell. This was the town where Kerouac grew up. George Martin and his wife, Marguerite, raise a large family of children. Like Leo Kerouac, George Martin is a printer. As critic Matt Theado wrote: "George hustles from his printing business to the horse races to big cigars . . . ," much like Leo Kerouac. "He possesses the high-energy traits that attracted Jack Kerouac throughout his career. George is gregarious and engaging and boisterous—a 'man's man' who is seen about town in restaurants and back-room poker games."[4]

Among the Martin children are four brothers—Joe, Francis, Peter and Mickey. These boys have some of the elements of Kerouac's own personality, and their lives include his own experiences. In one passage, Francis is described as "gloomy young Francis Martin," much like Kerouac himself.[5] Peter Martin becomes a successful high-school football player and wins a big game on Thanksgiving Day. As a result of his success, Peter receives a scholarship to college.

His older brother Joe, however, veers off in a different direction. He sees little purpose in life. "What's the use anyway? Who cares what happens!" he says to himself.[6] Like Kerouac, Joe wants to experience life, not spend his time studying books in college. One day, Joe announces to his stunned parents, "I'm gonna hit the road, Ma! I don't need any money!"[7] Joe eventually leaves home and begins hitchhiking to California, rather than go to college like his brother. While Joe leaves home, younger brother Mickey spends more time with his father. Kerouac creates a scene with Mickey and George Martin at the horse races. This was a scene that was probably similar to an experience Kerouac had enjoyed with his own father.

Unfortunately, George seems to spend too much time at the races and eventually loses his printing business. The family is forced to move to a cheap apartment, or tenement. Meanwhile, Francis Martin had won a scholarship to Harvard College in Cambridge, Massachusetts. One weekend when he returned home, Francis "suddenly saw with some misgivings how far down his family had had to go in order to maintain themselves and live. It seemed to him that the tenement . . . was a scene of spiritual deprivation, and even horror. . . . To see his own family living in what might well have been called the slums . . . was a fact that served to remind him how very close he might have come to such a life himself."[8]

Francis returned to Harvard. But Peter decided to drop out of college, following a football injury. He got a job to help support his family. Soon afterward, the

United States entered World War II. Joe Martin enlisted in the U.S. Army, while Peter joined the merchant marine. Peter's ship sailed across the Atlantic Ocean to Greenland. On the way back, however, another ship accompanying Peter's vessel was torpedoed and the sailors aboard it were drowned. As Kerouac wrote: "Men were strewn and lost a mile away on the ungodly waters, it was too much to fathom, too much to believe, no one knew what to think at all."[9] Kerouac experienced a similar incident while serving in the merchant marine, when a ship accompanying his vessel was torpedoed by a German submarine.

World War II combined with the Martins' financial problems helped to separate family members. Eventually, George and his wife moved to New York. This was the *City* mentioned in the book's title. Peter also began living in New York, which was far different from Galloway. As Kerouac wrote:

> He had known a boy's life in Galloway, he had grown up there and played football and lived in the big house with his family, he had known all the gravities and the glees and the wonders of life. Now all that was lost, vanished, haunted and ghostly—because it was no more.[10]

As he described the city experience, Kerouac repeatedly used words, such as, "furiously sad," "angry," "piteous," "something gleeful, rich and dark, something rare and wildly joyful."[11] Since his childhood, Kerouac had always been aware of the dark, sad side of life. This was due in part to the death of his brother. It was also an element of Jack Kerouac's personality. As his friend G. J. Apostolos put it, "Everything hurt the guy. Just a drizzly November day would zing him. I guess if you read his books, I guess somewhere you'd find the answer."[12]

In *The Town and the City*, Peter and Francis also moved to New York. Francis lived in Greenwich Village, popular with many artists and writers. Peter began hanging around with a group of people that included hoodlums and drug addicts. These were similar to the friends made by Kerouac while he lived in New York. Peter's parents, like Kerouac's own mother and father, did not like his friends when he brought them home. While Francis has very little to do with his parents, Peter continued to return to their home. George, his father, was dying, and Peter wanted to spend time with him.

> . . . This was the last life they would ever know each other in, and yet they wished they could live a hundred lives and do a thousand things and know each other forever in a million new ways. . . .[13]

George died at the end of the novel, leaving Peter feeling alone. He decided to leave New York and hit the road. "He was . . . traveling the continent westward, going off to further and further years, alone by the waters of life, alone . . . looking down along the shore in remembrance of the dearness of his father and of all life."[14] This ending seemed to foreshadow another novel that Kerouac had already begun that would be called *On the Road*.

Life Goes On

While Kerouac was writing his novel, his life in New York continued. Kerouac attended parties given by friends such as Allen Ginsberg. He also made several important new friends. One of them was Neal Cassady.

> **Kerouac attended parties given by friends such as Allen Ginsberg.**

He had traveled with his teenaged wife, Luanne Henderson, to visit an acquaintance in New York City, named Hal Chase. Chase was attending Columbia University and introduced Cassady to Kerouac.

During the summer of 1947, Kerouac left New York and headed to Denver by train to see Cassady. As he wrote his mother: "I've been eating apple pie & ice cream all over Iowa & Nebraska, where the food is so good."[15] By the time Kerouac reached Denver, Cassady and his wife had separated. Cassady had begun a relationship with another woman, Carolyn Robinson. Kerouac did not remain in Colorado for very long. He continued westward to San Francisco, hoping to find a job on a merchant marine ship. When no positions were available, he took a position as a security guard with a construction company.

Returning to New York City early in 1948, Kerouac began finishing *The Town and the City*. Then he painstakingly edited the long book and retyped it. On May 7, 1948, he wrote Cassady, "IT IS NOW FINISHED . . . IT IS IN THE HANDS OF SCRIBNER'S."[16]

Neal Cassady

Neal Cassady was born in Salt Lake City, Utah, on February 8, 1926. After his parents separated, Cassady lived with his father, a barber and an alcoholic. They moved around, living in run-down, seedy hotels, while Neal's father continued drinking.

Cassady was finally removed from his father by Catholic Charities in Denver, Colorado, and placed in a school for boys. However, Cassady received mostly poor grades in school and finally dropped out. To support himself, he began stealing cars. These thefts repeatedly landed him in jail. Kerouac was impressed with Cassady because he was willing to take risks and seemed not to care what others thought of him. Women found the handsome Cassady very attractive.

Kerouac also recognized that Cassady had superior intelligence, although he often seemed unwilling to use it. Nevertheless, Cassady wanted Kerouac to teach him how to write. Cassady's first trip to New York was brief, and he returned to the West in March 1947. However, Cassady and Kerouac had begun an important friendship that lasted for many years.

Neal Cassady is pictured driving his car with a female friend during the 1950s.

This meant that he had sent the novel to Scribner's Publishers—the same company that had published Thomas Wolfe's fiction. Kerouac hoped that Scribner's might pay him a large advance for the book.

But Scribner's turned down Kerouac's book. Other publishers also rejected it. Jack was very disappointed. As he wrote Neal Cassady late in 1948: ". . . I refuse to go on banking on the fantasy that I will make a living writing. Only charlatans, journalists, and phoneys do that. I'm through—although I'll go on writing."[17]

Meanwhile, Kerouac had returned to school. Anyone who had served in the armed forces during World War II was entitled to receive money from the federal government to pay for college. Under the GI Bill, Kerouac was paid seventy-five dollars or more each month. He used part of it to enroll in a college literature course and the rest to pay his bills.

Kerouac was not completely discouraged by the fact that his novel had not been accepted. In fact, he was still writing *On The Road*. Part of the material for the book came from a trip that Kerouac took with Neal Cassady early in 1949.

Success!

When Kerouac returned to New York, more rejection slips from publishers awaited him. Nevertheless, Kerouac's friends had faith in *The Town and the City*. He showed the manuscript to Allen Ginsberg, who praised it. Ginsberg also suggested that Kerouac send the manuscript to a Columbia professor named Mark

John Clellon Holmes

Among the friends made by Kerouac in New York during the late 1940s was John Clellon Holmes. Born in 1926 in Holyoke, Massachusetts, Holmes eventually moved to New York where he became a friend of Allen Ginsberg. In 1948, Holmes and Kerouac discussed a term that might describe their friends in New York. Kerouac called them the Beat Generation. By this he meant that they had been beaten down by the materialism of American society. They wanted to find something different, instead of working in nine-to-five jobs to pay for houses and automobiles.

Holmes later published a novel about the Beat Generation, a term that Holmes did not attribute to Kerouac, called *Go*. In 1952, he wrote an article for *The New York Times*, describing the Beat Generation. He described the term *beat* as meaning more "than weariness, it implies the feeling of having been used, of being raw." He went on to say that the Beat Generation had lived through a Depression and World War II. Therefore, they distrusted the values of conventional society, because they had led to these two terrible events. As Holmes put it, "*How* to live seems to them much more crucial than *why*." In other words, there seemed to be no conventional, materialistic goals worth striving for. Nevertheless, there "are the stirrings of a quest." The Beat Generation was looking for something, some reason for living, but they had not discovered what it was.[18]

Van Doren. Professor Van Doren liked the book. He called it "wiser than [Thomas] Wolfe."[19] Van Doren passed it along to a friend, Robert Giroux. Giroux was an editor at Harcourt Brace and Company, a major publishing company. Giroux was very impressed with *The Town and the City* and decided to publish it. Harcourt gave Kerouac an advance of one thousand dollars. This was not a large amount of money, but it helped Kerouac financially. As Kerouac wrote to one of his friends, "Well, boy, guess what? I sold my novel to Harcourt Brace . . . and got a $1,000 advance. . . . I feel good. My mother and family feel good. I am redeemed in so many ways that I realize now I've been living under a cloud of inferiority complex."[20]

Giroux recommended a number of editorial changes. He also persuaded Kerouac to shorten the book. Kerouac made many of these changes while he was on another trip across America. He traveled to Denver where he worked in a fruit market to help support himself. Kerouac had taken part of the money from his advance to bring his mother and sister out to Denver. He hoped that his mother would like the West and live there. But he was disappointed. After only a short time in Denver, she returned to New York. "I'd spent my $1,000 [money he had received as an advance] on . . . nothing," he wrote in his journal. "It seems that I have an infinite capacity to be unhappy."[21]

Kerouac returned to New York in the fall of 1949. He completed his work on *The Town and the City* with the help of Robert Giroux. The novel was finally published early in 1950. *The New York Times* called Kerouac "a brilliantly promising young novelist." *Newsweek* magazine added that Kerouac was "the best and most promising of the young novelists whose first works have recently appeared."[22] Harcourt sent Kerouac on a book tour to various cities to speak about his book. His stops included Denver and Lowell, Massachusetts. In his hometown, Kerouac signed copies of his book at a neighborhood bookstore. He was a local boy who had achieved his dream.

Chapter 5

No Easy Road to Success

Jack Kerouac had hoped that the publication of *The Town and the City* would enable him to achieve lasting success as a writer. As he wrote to his friend Neal Cassady, "when I 'published my book' . . . I thought I'd be rich."[1] But Kerouac was disappointed. Despite good reviews, the novel was not very popular and relatively few people bought it. With the popularity of black-and-white television sets, the epic novel was no longer widely read.

Nevertheless, Kerouac continued writing and, even more importantly, began experimenting with a new style. In part, this style arose out of his friendship with Neal Cassady. Cassady's method of speaking and writing was a nonstop stream of words with barely a breath in between. In his letters to Kerouac, Cassady poured out the story of his life. He hoped that someday he could publish his life's experiences as a book. After receiving one letter in December 1950, Kerouac wrote: "It was a

moment in lit. history when I received that thing. . . .
Ah man it's great. Don't undervalue your poolhall
musings, your excruciating details about streets,
appointment times, hotel rooms, bar locations, window
measurements, smells, heights of trees. I wait for you
to send me the entire thing in disorderly chronological
order anytime you say. . . ."[2]

Soon Kerouac's own style began to sound much
like Cassady's. As Kerouac's biographer Paul Maher
put it, "Jack had found his writing breakthrough . . .
[a] thirteen-thousand-word letter [from Cassady] . . . a
rambling scattershot narrative assaulting the reader
with its reckless verbosity."[3] One sentence read this
way: "There is a picture of me in a wickerbasket baby
carriage parked near the wall of a greystone garage in
Centralville . . . this is the name of the section of town
Lupine Road belonged . . . a picture of a plump crazy
baby, rather cute actually, sort of smiling at the world,
with a little hat on its head."[4]

In part of a letter, Kerouac wrote: "how I'm haunted
by the feeling that I am false. . . . I have renounced
fiction and fear. There is nothing to do but write the
truth. There is no other reason to write. I have to write
because of the compulsion in me. No more can I say.
I kneel before you in spirit and pray for honesty."[5]

Kerouac shared much of the information that passed
between him and Cassady with his second wife, Joan
Haverty. Kerouac met Joan in November 1950. She
had been the girlfriend of one of Kerouac's friends, Bill

Cannastra. However, Cannastra was killed in a tragic accident when he stuck his head out of the window of a speeding subway and bashed it against a steel pole. Kerouac and Joan Haverty conducted a whirlwind romance, and the couple married on November 17, 1950. After the marriage, they enjoyed a party with Allen Ginsberg, Lucien Carr, and John Clellon Holmes.

Kerouac continued to write but earned no income from his work. To cut expenses, the couple moved in with Kerouac's mother. Haverty also found a job at a department store. Friction developed between the couple, partly because Kerouac did nothing to bring in any income. Meanwhile, Gabrielle Kerouac seemed completely content with her son's lifestyle. Memere (similar to the French for grandmother), the name Kerouac called her, thought Haverty should stop complaining about her husband. Instead, she should recognize that he would eventually become a great writer.[6]

Gradually, the couple drifted apart. Haverty eventually made enough money to move out of Gabrielle Kerouac's home into her own apartment. Soon afterward, she told Kerouac that she was pregnant. He refused to believe that he was the father of the child and accused Haverty of having a relationship with another man. Early in 1952, Janet Michelle Kerouac was born. However, Kerouac did not recognize the baby as his child, refused to see her, and would not send Haverty any financial support for the little girl.

Working on New Fiction

While his marriage was falling apart, Kerouac continued to throw himself into writing. He was working on a writing experiment based on his conversations with a friend named Ed White, a local architect. Like other architects, White often made sketches of design concepts that appealed to him. These were quick drawings that could later be refined and turned into paintings. Kerouac began using a similar approach, called sketching, for his writing. He quickly wrote down his thoughts about something that he had experienced. It might be a café where he had eaten a meal in New York or a bar he visited during one of his trips on the road. Kerouac wrote quickly, pouring out his impressions in a continuous stream of language.

As Kerouac wrote to Allen Ginsberg:

Sketching (Ed White casually mentioned it in [a] . . .
Chinese restaurant near Columbia [University],
'Why don't you just sketch in the street like
a painter but with words') which I did . . .
everything activates in front of you in myriad
profusion, you just have to purify your mind
and let it pour the words . . . and write with
100% personal honesty . . . and slap it all down
nameless, willynilly, rapidly until sometimes I got
so inspired I lost consciousness I was writing.[7]

Since Kerouac was a very fast typist, sketching came more easily to him. Sketching also mirrored jazz, which Kerouac listened to so often in New York. Jazz musicians played a central theme in their music, then added improvisations that departed from the theme. Kerouac did the same thing in his writings. He started with a story, interrupting it with flashbacks and digressions, before coming back to the central story.

Visions of Cody

Many of these sketches appeared in Kerouac's new novel, *Visions of Cody*. The hero, Cody Pomeray, was actually based on Neal Cassady. The other main character in the novel was Jack Duluoz, based on Kerouac himself. Kerouac may have chosen the name Cody, after Buffalo Bill Cody. He was a famous nineteenth-century cowboy, known for his adventures in the West. Cody may have symbolized the cowboy independence that Kerouac associated with Neal Cassady. Visions may have suggested that Neal Cassady taught Kerouac "how to perceive," that is, how to see in a new way. This came from Cassady's own writing. Kerouac then wrote somewhat the same way that Cassady did.[8] *Visions of Cody* introduced Jack Duluoz and his family. They would appear in a series of other novels written by Kerouac later.

> **Cody may have symbolized the cowboy independence that Kerouac associated with Neal Cassady.**

At the beginning of the book, Kerouac introduced Cody Pomeray:

> This is an old diner like the ones Cody and his father ate in, long ago, with that oldfashioned railroad car ceiling and sliding doors—the board

where bread is cut is worn down fine as if with
bread dust and a plane; the icebox ("Say I got
some nice homefries tonight Cody!") is a huge
brownwood thing with oldfashioned pull-out
handles, windows, tile walls, full of lovely pans of
eggs, butter pats, piles of bacon—old lunchcarts
always have a dish of sliced raw onions ready to
go on hamburgs.[9]

This was an example of the sketches that Kerouac
had been writing.

Much of the first part of the book was filled with
Kerouac's descriptions of New York and thoughts
about Cody. In the second part of the book, Kerouac
described Cody's early life in Denver. In his biography
of Kerouac, Gerald Nicosia wrote that

[a] tie is established between the narrator [Jack
Duluoz] and his subject by revealing the heritage
of American memories they share. Jack and Cody
both grew up—gained their awareness of life—in
poor, red-brick cities. They are depicted as two
homeless, restless men, bound to keep moving. . . .
When they manage to escape the road, through
marriage for example, they must endure even
worse torments. But the identification between
Jack and Cody, which will grow stronger as the
book progresses, counters this negative field of
pain with the positive force of brotherhood.[10]

Kerouac then described the preparations made by
Duluoz to leave New York and visit Cody. In the next
part of the book, Kerouac included taped discussions
between the narrator and Cody. These were based
on "actual tapes Kerouac made with Cassady and

some of their friends," according to Nicosia. "The tapes introduce an intricate dovetailing of Cody's consciousness with Jack's. Telling each other their stories, the two main characters pool their perceptions and insights. Since they can now draw upon the same joint stock of knowledge and wisdom, they effectively become one mind."[11] The book also described the trips that Cassady and Kerouac had taken on the road. These descriptions were filled with their friends, the women they had met, and their experiences with drugs. Indeed, Kerouac and Cassady were smoking marijuana as they recorded their conversations on tape.

> **The book ended with Cody approaching his own death.**

In writing *Visions of Cody*, Kerouac used what is called a "nonlinear" writing style. That is, the book was not told in chronological order. It moved back and forth from the present to flashbacks of the past, and from transcripts of strict narrative to audio tapes of actual conversations between Kerouac and Cassady. The book ended with Cody approaching his own death:

> Goodbye Cody, your lips in your moments of self-possessed thought and new found responsible goodness are as silent, make as least a noise, and mystify with sense in nature, like the light of an automobile reflecting from the shiny silverpaint of a sidewalk tank this very instant, as silent and all this, as a bird crossing the dawn in search of the mountain cross and the sea beyond the city at the end of the land. Adios, you who watched the

sun go down, at the rail, by my side, smiling—
Adios, King.[12]

Cody and Jack Duluoz had established a close
friendship. This type of intimacy, Kerouac believed,
had disappeared from America. As Kerouac wrote:
"The sins of America are precisely that the streets . . .
are empty where their houses are, there's no sense
of neighborhood anymore. . . ."[13] In *Visions of Cody*,
Kerouac used a symbol to depict this sense of emptiness.
According to Gerald Nicosia, the symbol is

> [the] red brick hotel wall catching the glint of
> a red neon sign, which for Kerouac suggests, the
> intangible beauty and intimacy we always imagine
> on the inside of any world from which we are
> excluded, as if that hotel wall were being seen by
> some vagrant like Cody's father, too poor to rent
> a room. The real emotional content of the image,
> though, comes from the realization . . . that the
> magic is not there. . . .[14]

Kerouac's friend Allen Ginsberg later wrote: "Jack
Kerouac didn't write this book for money, he wrote it
for love, he gave it away to the world; not even for
fame, but as an explanation and prayer to his fellow
mortals. . . ."[15] However, the writing style was so
unusual that no publisher accepted the book after it was
completed. Indeed, Ginsberg did not like the book when
he first read it in 1952. As he wrote Kerouac: "I don't
see how it will ever be published. It's so personal, so
full of sex language. . . ."[16] In fact, *Visions of Cody* was
not published until after Kerouac's death and after he
had become famous for *On the Road*. By this time,

William S. Burroughs (left) and Jack Kerouac share a conversation
on a couch in New York City. Right around the time this photo
was taken, Burroughs was said to have been saying, "But Jack
I've told you over and over, if you continue your present pattern of
living with you memere [mother] you'll be wound closer and closer
in her apron strings till you're an old man."

Ginsberg's own view of Kerouac's writing had changed enormously.

Traveling Man

While Kerouac was working on *Visions of Cody*, he suffered an attack of phlebitis. This is an inflammation of the veins in his legs. Jack traveled to North Carolina. His sister, Nin, and her husband were living there. Gabrielle Kerouac had also traveled there from New York to visit her daughter. However, the phlebitis grew worse, and Kerouac eventually came back to New York and went into the hospital for two months. After his recovery, Kerouac hoped to get a job on a merchant marine vessel. But the ship left without him. With money from a friend named Henri Cru, Kerouac traveled to southern California, hoping to find another merchant marine job. But there was not one available. So Kerouac traveled north to San Francisco, where Cassady was living with his wife, Carolyn.

Cassady helped Kerouac find a job as a baggage handler on the railroad.

Cassady, who was employed by the Southern Pacific Railroad, helped Kerouac find a job as a baggage handler on the railroad. Meanwhile, Kerouac finished *Visions of Cody*. He also helped Cassady with his own book, *The First Third*. While living with the Cassadys, Kerouac began having a love affair with Cassady's wife, Carolyn. According to Kerouac's biographer Tom Clark, the situation created too much tension in the relationship between Cassady and Kerouac. According to Clark, "He and Neal were fighting for the first time in their lives. . . ."[17]

Kerouac decided to leave San Francisco and visit William S. Burroughs, who was living in Mexico City, the capital of Mexico. In 1951, Burroughs had accidentally killed his wife, Joan, during a party. Burroughs had put a glass on her head and tried to shoot it off with a gun. Unfortunately, the bullet hit Joan and she died. Kerouac traveled partway to Mexico City with the Cassadys, who left him at the Mexican border. Kerouac hopped a bus that took him the rest of the way to Mexico City. He smoked pot along the way and tried a new drug, peyote. This is a hallucinogenic drug that enables users to see strange visions. Eventually, Kerouac reached Burroughs' home in Mexico City. Shortly after his arrival, the two men went to see a bullfight. But Jack was appalled by what he saw. The sight of the bull being killed sickened him. "And I saw how everybody dies and nobody's going to care," Kerouac wrote. "I felt how awful it is to live just so you can die like a bull trapped in a screaming human ring."[18]

Dr. Sax

While he was staying with Burroughs in Mexico, Kerouac was working on another book. He called this book *Dr. Sax*. The novel began with Jack Duluoz growing up in Lowell, Massachusetts. In the opening of the novel, Kerouac described Lowell:

> In the dream of the wrinkly tar corner I saw it, hauntingly, Riverside Street as it ran across Moody

> and into the fabulously rich darknesses of Sarah
> Avenue and Rosemont the Mysterious . . .
> Rosemont:—community built in the floodable river
> flats and also on gentle slopes uprising that to the
> foot of the sandbank, the cemetery meadows and
> haunted ghostfields of . . . hermits and Mill Pond
> so mad. . . .[19]

While he was growing up, Jack Duluoz encountered death repeatedly. His brother died and his childhood friend Zap Plouffe was killed by a heavy wagon. Duluoz also lived through the terrible flood of the Merrimack River that destroyed part of Lowell and killed some of its citizens.

In Lowell, Duluoz encountered the mysterious Dr. Sax. According to Duluoz, "Doctor Sax was like The Shadow when I was young, I saw him leap over the last bush on the sandbank one night, cape a-flying. . . ."[20] This character was roughly based on William S. Burroughs. Sax was involved in a titanic struggle against a large snake. This snake was the symbol of evil and death. In the last part of the book, Duluoz and Dr. Sax encountered the giant snake as they looked down at him from the walls of a huge castle:

> . . . I began to look, I said to myself "This is a
> Snake" and when the consciousness of the fact
> that it was a snake came over me and I began to
> look at its two great lakes of eyes I found myself
> looking into the horror, into the void, I found
> myself looking into the Dark, I found myself
> looking into IT, I found myself compelled to fall.[21]

Dr. Sax tried to destroy the snake by pouring a magic

potion on it. But the snake was not stopped until a large bird appeared to carry it away. "It was such a big bird that when it flapped and flew with a mighty slowmotion in the tragic shrunken sky it was like watching waves of great black water going C-r-a-s-h with a heavy slowness against gigantic icebergs ten miles away, but up in the air and upside down and awful."[22]

Although Sax has failed, the snake was gone:

> And Doctor Sax, standing there with his hands in his pockets, his mouth dropped open, uptilted his searching profile into the enigmatic sky— made a fool of—"I'll be damned," he said with amazement. "The Universe disposes of its own evil."[23]

In *Dr. Sax*, Kerouac moved back and forth from fantasy to reality. It was a new type of writing for him. Kerouac sent a copy of *Dr. Sax* to Allen Ginsberg, who praised the book. As Kerouac wrote him: "I read your letter many times. It's very nice, you are very nice to understand my writings. I felt honored."[24] Kerouac left Mexico and headed west to spend some time with Neal Cassady. Although Cassady and Kerouac had experienced a falling out over Carolyn Cassady, the two old friends had eventually made up. Kerouac went back to work on the railroad. He also read Cassady excerpts of *Dr. Sax*. But the relationship between the two men gradually grew worse once again. In fact, it had never recovered after Kerouac's affair with Carolyn Cassady. Kerouac moved out of the Cassadys' house into his own run-down room in a local hotel. Kerouac traveled back to Mexico City. After a brief stay with Burroughs, he returned to New York.

Although he had high hopes for *Dr. Sax*, no publisher wanted it. An editor at one publishing company told him that the material on Lowell was good. However, the fantasy material involving Doctor Sax, the editor said, had no market. Except for one published novel, Kerouac's literary efforts had produced only failure.

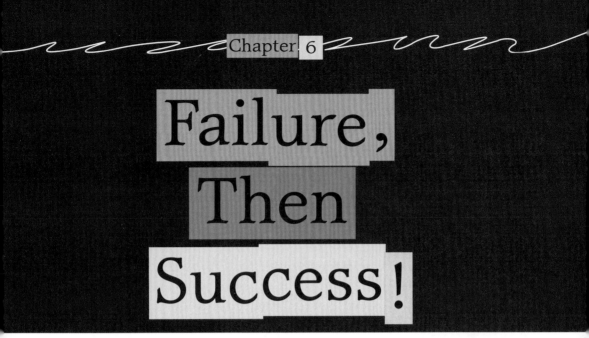

Chapter 6

Failure,
Then
Success!

Although Jack Kerouac had only published one novel, he did not give up on his efforts to become a successful writer. Nevertheless, it was becoming more difficult for him to keep going. As he looked around, Kerouac saw that some of his friends were having more success than he had achieved.

In 1952, his friend John Clellon Holmes had published the novel *Go*. This was considered the first published book of the Beat Generation. In his novel, Holmes wrote that the Beat Generation had been greatly inspired by jazz:

> In this modern jazz, they heard something rebel and nameless that spoke for them, and their lives knew a gospel for the first time. It was more than a music; it became an attitude toward life, a way of walking, a language and a costume; and these introverted kids . . . now felt somewhere at last.[1]

Kerouac was jealous of the fact that Holmes was now

a recognized author who "made $20,000 on GO." In a letter to Neal Cassady, Kerouac wrote: "Holmes . . . eats in expensive restaurants and spends all his time chasing and hailing cabs. . . . everybody's in his heaven, God made the world, I'm okay too and get hi once a night and still believe and still love you."[2] Holmes knew how Kerouac felt about his success. As Holmes later said, ". . . he was angry at me. Not angry at me perhaps, but angry that I'd broken through in a way that he really wanted to." Nevertheless, Holmes's feelings for Jack did not change. "I *liked* Jack, at times almost like a brother, someone I knew very well. We used to walk a lot, and sometimes we just goofed, sat around and talked and did nothing."[3]

> "I *liked* Jack, at times almost like a brother, someone I knew very well."

Meanwhile, Kerouac was working on a new book. He called it *Maggie Cassidy*. In this novel, which is part of the Duluoz legend, Kerouac returned to Lowell. The book was based on his romance with Mary Carney. However, the title of the novel probably also referred to Carolyn Cassady, whom Kerouac loved.[4]

In the first part of the novel, Kerouac described Lowell and the Merrimack River, much as he had in *The Town and the City*. Maggie and her family represented the stable life of Lowell. Unlike the Beats, her father, James Cassidy, went to work each day and returned to his family each night. He symbolized the stable routine of family life in a small town. Maggie grew up, hoping to repeat this same lifestyle. She and "Jackie" Duluoz fell in love and enjoyed the romance of young people who hoped to spend their lives together. However, Duluoz had other plans. Much like Kerouac, he wanted to leave Lowell for college and what he believed would be a more exciting life in New York City.

Duluoz went to New York, but eventually he returned to Lowell and tried to resume his romance with Maggie. Although he bragged about his worldly experiences in New York, she was no longer interested in him. Duluoz has become "cold hearted," Maggie said, and any romance between them was over.[5]

Traveling Again

After working on *Maggie Cassidy*, Kerouac decided to leave New York and head to California again to visit the Cassadys. In fact, Cassady had arranged a job for Kerouac on the railroad. From California, Kerouac wrote his mother and invited her to come out for a visit. "I'll lay off work & show you around," he said.[6] Jack continued his close relationship with Memere and worried about her living alone in New York. However, instead of coming to California, she preferred to visit her daughter, Nin, in North Carolina.

Kerouac soon grew bored with the railroad job. He left and took a position on a merchant marine ship, the S.S. *William Carruth*. The ship was headed for Alabama and the East Coast. According to Kerouac's biographer Gerald Nicosia, Jack lay on the ship's deck at night studying the stars. "When the ship docked in Mobile

[Alabama] in late June, he got drunk with a prostitute and was caught strolling . . . with her down Main Street when he should have been working. Facing reprimand, he agreed to quit when the ship reached New Orleans."[7]

Kerouac left the *Carruth* and returned to New York. There he visited with Allen Ginsberg and William S. Burroughs. Kerouac also began a love affair with a woman named Alene Lee. She was part African American and part American Indian. Kerouac was introduced to Lee at a party. She had suffered a nervous breakdown previously and was currently in therapy to deal with her emotional problems. Lee told him all about her breakdown because she "felt Jack's sympathy so strongly," according to biographer Gerald Nicosia. Kerouac loved her "for the honesty and clarity" that she used to tell him about her life.[8] When he was not spending time with Lee, Kerouac was writing short pieces about his experiences on the railroad in California.

The Subterraneans

Kerouac's relationship with Alene Lee was very short. Their major common interest was jazz, but little else. Lee was not interested in a long-term relationship, nor was Kerouac. Nevertheless, in October 1953, she became one of the main characters in Kerouac's new novel, *The Subterraneans*. The title describes a group of Kerouac's friends in New York City. They were artists, writers, and musicians, part of the Beat Generation. Some of them used drugs.

Kerouac makes a face at the camera while walking along east Seventh Street, past Tompkins Square Park in New York City.

Instead of setting the story in New York, Kerouac chose San Francisco. One reason, according to critic Matt Theado, was to "maintain the anonymity of his characters—especially of Alene Lee, who did not wish to be identified. . . ."[9] She is known as Mardou Fox in the book, and the male character—representing Kerouac—is called Leo Percepied.

On the first page of the book, Kerouac described the *Subterraneans* as "hip without being slick, they are intelligent without being corny, they are intellectual . . . without being pretentious . . . they are very quiet. . . ."[10] Much of the book described the relationship between Leo and Mardou Fox. Mardou accused Leo and other men of being incapable of forming relationships. "Men are so crazy," she said, "they want the essence, the woman is the essence, there it is right there in their hands. . . . Instead they rush off and have big wars and consider women as prizes instead of human beings, well man I may be in the middle of all this . . . but I certainly don't want any part of it. . . ."[11]

Leo admitted in the novel that his writing—his work—"was my dominant thought, not love." He believed that love brought pain, because he was constantly forced to choose between Mardou and his work.[12] When Leo wanted to write, Mardou wanted him to spend time with her. Mardou also resented Leo's relationship with his mother where he seemed to spend more time than he did with her. "But why do you always want to rush off so soon?" she asked him. "I guess a feeling of well-being at home," Leo answered. "I know baby," she replied, "but I'm, I miss you in a way I'm jealous that you have a home and a mother who irons your clothes and all that and I haven't—."[13]

Eventually, the relationship between Leo and Mardou ended. The early days of love disappeared. Leo wanted Mardou to go so he could "stay at home all week and write and work on the three novels to make a lot of money and come in to town only for good times if not to see Mardou then any other chick will do. . . ."[14] Mardou also wanted her independence from Leo. At the end of the book, Kerouac wrote: "And I go home having lost her love. And write this book."[15] He realized that instead of a long-term relationship, he had substituted the process of writing about it.

Kerouac had trouble convincing editors to accept his style of writing.

Although Burroughs was impressed with Kerouac's new work, no publisher was interested in publishing it. Meanwhile, Kerouac was also trying to interest an editor at Viking Publishers in his other works, such as *On the Road*. But Malcolm Cowley, the Viking editor, told Kerouac that large parts of the novel would have to be cut before the novel could be published.

Kerouac had trouble convincing editors to accept his style of writing. Nevertheless, he refused to change it. Kerouac's approach to writing was similar to the way some of his artist friends approached painting. Among them were artist Jackson Pollock and Willem de

Writing *The Subterraneans*

The Subterraneans is a short novel, just over one hundred pages. Kerouac wrote it in three days, while he was taking Benzedrine. It was written in a stream of consciousness style. That is, the sentences run on for many words in a way that is similar to a writer's thoughts. Kerouac also compared the writing style to bebop. The sentences were punctuated with digressions and asides, like the improvisations in jazz. Here is an example:

> I was coming down the street with Larry O'Hara drinking buddy of mine from all the times in San Francisco in my long and nervous and mad careers I've gotten drunk and in fact cadged drinks off friends with such "genial" regularity nobody really cared to notice or announce that I am developing or was developing, in my youth, such bad freeloading habits though of course they did notice but liked me.[16]

Soon after finishing the novel, Kerouac described the approach that he had used to write it to his friends Allen Ginsberg and William S. Burroughs. He called this process "Spontaneous Prose":

> Set Up: The object is set before the mind, either in reality, as in sketching . . . or is set in the memory wherein it becomes the sketching from memory of a definite image-object. Procedure: Time being of the essence in the purity of speech, sketching language is undisturbed flow from the mind of personal secret idea-words, blowing (as per jazz musician) on subject of image.

> Method: No periods separating sentence-structures already arbitrarily riddled by false colons and timid usually needless comas—but the vigorous space dash separating rhetorical breathing (as jazz musician drawing breath between outblown phrases).[17]

Kooning. They represented a new style of art called "abstract expressionism." Pollock believed that painting "was not preconceived, but flowed out of the painter's spontaneous muscular gestures." This was similar to Jack's spontaneous writing. Many of Pollock's paintings were developed using the drip style. He dripped spots of paint onto his canvas with spontaneous movements of his paintbrush.[18]

Although Kerouac believed in his style of writing, he was discouraged by the constant rejections from publishers. Therefore, he decided to head west again to visit the Cassadys. Neal had found a job for Kerouac— working as a parking lot attendant. However, Kerouac's stay with the Cassadys was short. Cassady and Kerouac had an argument over how they should split up a pile of marijuana. Kerouac moved out and took an apartment on his own. A short time later, he returned to New York and moved back in with his mother.

Approaching Success

Although Kerouac did not realize it, his major breakthrough was getting closer. In spring 1954, Kerouac's friend Robert Giroux had helped him find a new literary agent. His name was Sterling Lord. Generally, an agent's contacts helped a writer sell his books. Although Kerouac had worked with agents in the past, they had not been successful in selling most of his novels.

Sterling Lord began submitting *Maggie Cassidy*, *Visions of Cody*, *Dr. Sax*, and *The Subterraneans*. Lord

73

also sent out copies of *On the Road*, which was re-titled *The Beat Generation*. Meanwhile, Lord and Malcolm Cowley had arranged for the publication of an excerpt from *On the Road* in a magazine. The essay was called "Jazz of the Beat Generation." Kerouac did not publish the essay under his own name. He was concerned that his former wife, Joan Haverty, might find out about it. Then she might try to obtain some of the money he received from writing the article.[19] Haverty wanted money for child support for Janet, whom she claimed was their daughter. Indeed, Haverty sued Kerouac for child support in 1954, and he was arrested in December. Kerouac was later brought into court. However, his lawyer argued that he was unable to work because of his recurring attacks of phlebitis. The judge decided to suspend the case so Kerouac would not be forced to support Janet.

> **By early 1955, the publication of his essay was the only good news that Kerouac had received.**

By early 1955, the publication of his essay was the only good news that Kerouac had received. As he wrote Malcolm Cowley: "This is the first, the only break into print for me outside of TOWN AND CITY. It gives me a lift towards further effort; I'd begun to lose heart. Thank you ever so much."[20]

But the article paid very little money. Cowley also found another magazine that agreed to publish an excerpt from *On the Road*. But the magazine paid only fifty dollars for the article.

Kerouac's other books, including *The Subterranneans*, had been rejected. In the meantime, Kerouac's mother had decided to leave her job and move south to live with Nin in North Carolina. Kerouac went with her because he did not have any money to support himself in New York. He spent part of the summer in North Carolina and then hitchhiked to Mexico. Kerouac stayed in a friend's apartment in Mexico City, where he wrote poetry. During this period, Kerouac composed his poem, "Mexico City Blues."

The poem was written in 242 parts, called choruses; just as Kerouac said. Kerouac never forgot his brother, Gerard, and mentioned him in the poem. He also remained a devout Catholic, never straying far from his belief in Christ. For this reason, he made biblical references in "Mexico City Blues."[21] Also, in one chorus Kerouac summed up his Beat style of life.[22]

Beat Poets in San Francisco

In the fall, Kerouac left Mexico City and traveled to California. His old friend Allen Ginsberg was living in Berkeley, a town near San Francisco. Ginsberg invited Kerouac to a reading of his new poem at a place called the Six Gallery. Ginsberg called his poem "Howl." Jack was the master of ceremonies for the event. The poetry reading was greeted with applause by the large audience who attended the event. The reading, on October 13, 1955, marked the birth of the San Francisco Renaissance. The following year, the poem was published.

Allen Ginsberg speaks at a rally in Berkeley, California, on July 30, 1965. While reciting a poem, he crashed tiny cymbals together.

"Howl"

As critic Ann Charters wrote, Allen Ginsberg was inspired by a poem written by Jack Kerouac—"Mexico City Blues." It helped Ginsberg "to begin to type what he called his most personal 'imaginative sympathies' in the long poem 'Howl for Carl Solomon.'"[23] This poem presents some of the major themes of the Beat Generation.

As Ginsberg later said in an interview, "Kerouac persuaded me to stop writing rhyme poems and revising everything fifty thousand times; to just lay it out on the page in the sequence of thought-forms that arise in my mind during the time of composition."[24] Ginsberg's poem and the gathering at the Six Gallery marked the beginning of a poetry renaissance in San Francisco. Some of the other poets at the reading became very well known. Among them was Gary Snyder, who became a friend of Jack Kerouac.

Kerouac remained in California during much of the fall and then traveled to North Carolina to live with his sister and mother. Kerouac enjoyed spending his time with his nephew, Nin's son, Paul. He even taught him the finer points of football.

But Kerouac did not stay in one place for very long. With money from his mother, Kerouac headed west again in 1956. Poet Gary Snyder had arranged a job for Kerouac as a lookout in the Cascade Mountains of Washington. Snyder loved the outdoors and spent much of his time hiking through the wilderness. Kerouac was supposed to spot any forest fires and alert people who would try to stop them. As he wrote Lucien Carr:

> I'm assigned to do my fire-spotting this summer
> on top of Desolation Peak in the Primitive Area
> of Mt. Baker National Forest . . . 12 miles south
> of British Columbia wilds. Wow, I'm all set to
> go. . . . I'll be trained . . . a week and then up the
> mountain I go with an Indian and his burro-team,
> with 2 months' supply of food, to the shack,
> where he leaves me, glory be.[25]

This was only a summer job. But Kerouac soon grew bored living alone in the mountains, watching for fires, and writing in his notebooks. He enjoyed the company of other people as a relief from the solitary occupation of writing. This was one of the reasons why Kerouac spent time living with his mother and his sister. He also liked visiting friends such as the Cassadys and Allen Ginsberg, as well as hanging out in bars and nightclubs

While on firewatch, Kerouac was able to see beautiful views in the Cascade Mountains.

with other artists. After the job was over, Kerouac left the mountains and headed for San Francisco.

Meanwhile, pictures of Ginsberg and some of his friends had begun appearing in major magazines and newspapers in the United States. Ginsberg, Kerouac, and others were being hailed as a new generation of poets and writers. Then, in early December, came the news that Kerouac had most hoped to hear. Viking Publishers had decided to publish *On the Road*. Suddenly, Kerouac's entire life was about to change.

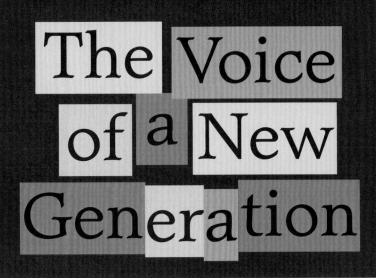

Chapter 7

The Voice of a New Generation

Over the next few years, Jack Kerouac continued to travel, increased his spiritual awareness, and finally achieved success. Kerouac became the voice of the Beat Generation. But he also discovered that success was not exactly what he had expected.

Early in 1957, Jack traveled to Tangier, Morocco, in North Africa. In one of his later novels, *Desolation Angels*, begun about this time, Kerouac wrote:

> Then like seeing sudden slow files of Mohammedan women in white I saw the white roofs of the little port of Tangier sitting right there in the elbow of the land, on the water. This dream of white robed Africa on the blue afternoon Sea, wow, who dreamed it? . . . White sheets waving on the rooftop![1]

He had gone there to visit his old friend William S. Burroughs. While living in Tangier, Burroughs was working on a new novel. Kerouac helped Burroughs edit his new book and even typed part of the manuscript. Kerouac also came up with a new name for the novel, *Naked Lunch*.

Kerouac was joined in Tangier by Allen Ginsberg, who also helped with the book. After about a month, however, Kerouac had grown tired of Tangier. He left Morocco and traveled to Paris. In the meantime, he had received an advance for *On the Road*. Therefore, he could afford to spend time seeing the beautiful churches, walking in the parks, and visiting the museums of Paris. It was the first time Kerouac had seen the city. From Paris, Jack went to London, where *On the Road* had been sold to a European publisher. He picked up a check for the advance. Then, he returned to New York and headed for Florida. His mother as well as his sister and her husband were living in Orlando. Kerouac had sent much of the money from his advance to his mother to help support her.

However, Kerouac did not enjoy the warm, humid weather in Florida and soon left for California. Kerouac loved California and wanted his mother to live out there with him. He paid to move her out there. However, she did not like California; she was too far away from Nin and her grandchild. Once again, Kerouac had spent much of the money from his advance in a failed attempt to create a new home for his mother and himself. Jack gave up on his dream of creating a home in California. Instead, he brought his mother back to Florida and helped her move into a new apartment.

Naked Lunch

In *Naked Lunch*, Burroughs combined the elements of fiction and science fiction. The book describes the lifestyle of urban criminals, as well as the subculture of drugs. Burroughs had been heavily dependent on drugs for many years. Indeed, he wrote *Naked Lunch* while taking large doses of morphine. This is a powerful narcotic and is dangerous if not used under the supervision of a doctor. However, while he was in Tangier, Burroughs managed to end his dependence on morphine with the help of doctors there.

After *Naked Lunch* was published in 1959, it became very popular, especially among some young people in America. Critic Paul Kane described the novel as "a collection of very loosely related incidents and anecdotes," with no structure or conventional plot. ". . . [M]uch of the 180 or so pages is taken up with descriptions of drug-buying, drug-taking . . . the paranoia of being caught doing these things, and the efforts of the medical profession to tackle or control (a central theme) the problem of addiction."[2] Much of the book is also filled with sex, one of the reasons that it was banned in several states because some people felt it was too obscene.

On the Road

> With the coming of Dean Moriarty began the
> part of my life you could call my life on the road.
> Before that I'd often dreamed of going West to see
> the country, always vaguely planning and never
> taking off. Dean is the perfect guy for the road
> because he was actually born on the road, when his
> parents were passing through Salt Lake City. . . .[3]

With these words, Jack Kerouac began *On the Road*.

Jack Kerouac was not an overnight success. In fact, he had begun writing *On the Road* in 1948—more than ten years before it was finally published. Kerouac wrote and rewrote his novel many times. He kept a record of his efforts in a series of journals. These were spiral notebooks, each six inches by nine and one half inches. Kerouac often wrote in the middle of the night. Frequently, he wrote for hours at a single sitting. Kerouac could type very quickly. Words poured onto the paper from his typewriter, as he composed chapter after chapter of his novels.

On the Road went through many variations. At one point, in 1949, Kerouac called the novel the *Hip Generation*. Later he changed the name to *The Beat Generation*. Finally, he settled on the title by which it became famous, *On the Road*. At first, the book's hero was named Red Moultrie. Moultrie was a minor-league baseball player. He had also been a truck driver and a jazz musician. Eventually Kerouac changed the hero's name to Dean Moriarty. This character was based on Kerouac's close friend Neal Cassady. Cassady appealed to Kerouac, because he was free and willing to take risks. He did not tie himself to a regular job. Instead, he spent much of his time traveling around America. Moriarty's sidekick, Sal Paradise, narrates the novel and is based on Kerouac.

In addition to Moriarty and Paradise, Kerouac filled the story with characters based on his other beat friends. They included a character based on Allen Ginsberg. This character was called Carlo Marx in the novel. Another character was based on William S. Burroughs. He was called Old Bull Lee in the novel. Kerouac also included Cassady's wife, Carolyn, a beautiful blonde woman. She was called Camille in the novel.

He typed the manuscript on several long sheets of paper taped together.

In 1951, Kerouac typed out an entire draft of *On the Road* in approximately three weeks. He typed the manuscript on several long sheets of paper taped together. Each page was connected so Kerouac did not need to stop at the bottom of one page, insert another page in the typewriter, and continue typing. After completing his work, Kerouac took the manuscript to Robert Giroux. Giroux was an editor at Harcourt Publishers, which had published Kerouac's first novel. Kerouac handed the scroll to Giroux, who pushed it away. "How can we edit a thing like that?" he said.[4]

The Struggle Continues

Kerouac was very upset. He left the office and stopped working with Giroux. But he did not give up on his

The scroll on which Kerouac first wrote *On the Road* has become a collector's item. Here, Jim Irsay, owner of the Indianapolis Colts, talks about his purchase of the scroll in 2004 for $2.43 million.

novel. He kept writing more drafts of *On the Road*. Kerouac thought he had been destined by God to be a writer. Kerouac had grown up with a very strong Catholic faith, given to him by his parents. He believed strongly that "I belong to God and am working blindly at His Bright Bidding, according to *His Intentions*," as he wrote in his journal.[5] Sometimes Kerouac got stuck and could not figure out where to take his story. But he did not abandon the project. Instead, he put the novel away, worked on something else, and then went back to it again.

Kerouac wanted to bring the people to life whom he had met during his travels. Since he had little money, Kerouac often took buses along the roads or hitchhiked. He met truck drivers, stopped at seedy hotels, went to bars, talked to homeless people, and listened to jazz musicians. These were the people whom he portrayed in his novel along with his friends in the Beat Generation. Most novelists had never written about these people. Americans in the 1940s and 1950s felt that the homeless people Jack met on his travels were failures. Publishers generally agreed that people were really not interested in reading about the homeless. They believed that most of their readers would not care about the characters that Kerouac included in his novel.

In 1951, Kerouac finally received a break. A small publishing company, A. A. Wyn, gave him a small advance for *On the Road*. Kerouac used the money to take a trip from New York, on the road. Unfortunately,

Wyn changed its mind about the novel. In 1952, the publisher told Kerouac that the writing style was too different and unusual to appeal to most readers. Kerouac went out west to visit his friends, Neal and Carolyn Cassady. The Cassadys gave him their support because they believed in Kerouac's talent as a writer.

Kerouac did not give up on the novel. But in 1953, it was rejected by another publisher. By this time, Kerouac had contacted Malcolm Cowley. Cowley, an editor at Viking Publishers, liked the book. Eventually, he arranged to get small parts of the book published in several magazines. Readers liked what they saw. Viking Publishers had also begun to share Cowley's faith in the novel. However, Viking's lawyers were concerned that the publisher might get sued by the people on whom Kerouac based his characters. The characters were described taking drugs and having love affairs; this might cause a scandal. Therefore, Kerouac used fictitious names for all of his real characters. He also obtained signed agreements from people such as Cassady and Ginsberg. The agreements stated that they would not sue the publisher for what was written in the novel. Finally, in 1957, Viking published *On the Road*.

> **Kerouac did not give up on the novel.**

The original manuscript of four hundred fifty pages had been reduced by more than one hundred pages. According to scholar Matt Theado, "Apparently the changes that he [Kerouac] made at Viking's request came mostly in the form of cuts, insertions, punctuation changes, and the alterations of characters to hide their real-life identities." Kerouac later said that Cowley had forced him to put in many punctuation marks, such as commas, to make the sentences easier to read. However, Cowley stated that he had done no such thing. Nevertheless, as Theado pointed out, "An excerpt from *On the Road* published in . . . April 1955 gives readers an opportunity to see what the prose of the book may have looked like before Viking's editing. Titled 'Jazz of the Beat Generation,' the excerpt corresponds to approximately ten pages of *On the Road* and employs forty fewer commas."[6]

The Story

When the story in *On the Road* begins, Sal Paradise was on a college campus. He had also briefly been married, but "my wife and I split up."[7] By his own admission, "everything was dead." After meeting Moriarty, however, Paradise found himself wanting to go on the road, just as Moriarty was doing—"beginning to get the bug like Dean."[8] These words reflected Kerouac's own feelings after he had met Neal Cassady, who helped convince Jack Kerouac to leave New York and travel to experience America.

In Part I of *On the Road*, Moriarty returns to the West without Paradise. But Paradise does not give up his desire to travel and meet new people. Much of his desire for these experiences is based on his desire to write about them in his novels. Like Kerouac, Paradise is a writer who wants to use his own adventures as material for his stories. As Paradise puts it in the novel, "I shambled after [them] as I've been doing all my life after people who interest me, because the only people for me are the mad ones, the ones who are mad to live, mad to talk, mad to be saved . . . burn, burn, burn like fabulous yellow roman candles. . . ."[9]

This sentence accurately described the members of the Beat Generation. They appealed to many young readers of Kerouac's book in the 1950s. Some of them had served in World War II. They had seen hundreds of their friends killed or wounded. They wanted to escape from their memories of the past into something new. Many were looking for more than nine-to-five jobs or a home in the suburbs. Kerouac and the Beats offered them an alternative. The Beats also provided young college students with something new. Many of them wanted to rebel from their parents' conventional lifestyles. *On the Road* seemed to provide the answer.

> ". . . the only people for me are the mad ones . . ."

Paradise travels west to Denver, Colorado, where he finds Moriarty and Carlo Marx. There Paradise experiences the exciting city life of Denver. He also goes out into the beautiful Rocky Mountains. Paradise also begins a series of love affairs with women who appear in the novel. One of them, Rita Bettencourt, seems to have little purpose in life. Kerouac contrasted the sadness experienced by many people in life with Paradise's own excitement being on the road with Dean Moriarty and his friends. Those people had settled for a conventional lifestyle, Paradise is reaching for something more. From Denver, Paradise heads to San Francisco and Los Angeles, and then returns to New York City.

Part II of the novel begins a year later when Dean Moriarty travels to Virginia and New York City. Moriarty had left his wife and baby daughter, spent all his money on a new car, and driven east. By the time Moriarty reaches New York, he is broke. Lack of money, however, does not prevent Moriarty and Paradise from beginning a trip on the road.

In Part II, the travelers head south to Florida, across the Gulf Coast, and on to Louisiana. In Algiers, Louisiana, they encounter an old friend—Old Bull Lee. Lee is portrayed as a strange eccentric, who had traveled to Europe and to many cities in America. Along the way, Lee, like William S. Burroughs, had become a heavy drug user. Eventually, Moriarty and Paradise leave Bull Lee and head to Texas, finally reaching California.

Along the way, they encounter a variety of attractive women. Many of the women who appeal to Paradise are Mexican or African American. He spends more than two weeks with a Mexican girl, Terry. Paradise is interested in more than white America, where he grew up. He wants to experience the world of minority groups, like Hispanic and African Americans. Much of his interest also focuses on jazz, which is primarily played by African-American musicians.

The Beats found 1950s white America too homogeneous—that is, it was too much alike. During the fifties, America was still a segregated nation. African Americans and other minority groups lived apart from whites. Most white Americans did not venture into minority neighborhoods. The Beats rebelled against this type of culture. Kerouac developed close friendships with African Americans. He believed that the American experience included all racial groups, not just whites.

During much of their travels together, which continue in Part III, Moriarty and Paradise are searching for "It." Although this is a difficult concept to explain, it seems to mean living in the moment. Moriarty seems uninterested in any long-term goals, only enjoying life as it happens. He compares this experience to the music of jazz musicians. "The key moment, Dean says, is when time stops and the musician draws upon the material of everyone's lives to fill the vacuum that surrounds them," according to critic Matt Theado.[10]

He believed that the American experience included all racial groups, not just whites.

While Moriarty lives for the moment, Paradise is looking for something else. Much of the driving force behind his travels is to find material for a book. Paradise begins Part IV with, "I came into some money from selling my book. . . ."[11] This is similar to Kerouac's experience selling *The Town and the City*. Paradise uses this money to begin another trip with Moriarty. This time they travel southward to Mexico City, which Kerouac himself had visited. Although Paradise is thinking about his writing, he still wants to, in Moriarty's words, experience "and *understand* the world as, really and genuinely speaking, other Americans haven't done before us. . . ."[12] Like Paradise, Kerouac was looking for something off the beaten path. He had moved away from the traditional way of living.

However, Paradise soon ends his travels and returns to New York. He eventually settles down with another woman. But Moriarty's travels continue. As Kerouac wrote at the end of the novel:

> So in America when the sun goes down and I sit on the old broken-down river pier watching the long, long skies over New Jersey . . . which is just before the coming of complete night that blesses the earth, darkens all rivers, cups the peaks and folds the final shore in, and nobody, nobody knows what's going to happen to anybody besides the forlorn rags of growing old, I think of Dean Moriarty. . . .[13]

When *On the Road* was published it was hailed as "the novel that defined a generation." Critic Aaron Latham, writing in *The New York Times*, called it the *Huckleberry Finn* of the mid-twentieth century. "Kerouac substituted the road for the river, the fast car for the slow raft [that Huck and the slave Jim took along the Mississippi River in the nineteenth century] the hipster in search of freedom for the black slave in search of freedom. . . ."[14]

Indeed, author Bruce Cook added that Kerouac was carrying on a tradition started by Mark Twain. In *Huckleberry Finn*, Jim and Huck were searching for freedom. Jim, the black slave, wanted to escape from slavery. Huck was trying to escape from his life with Aunt Sally. She wanted him to live by conventional middle-class values, and Huck wanted nothing of it. As Huck said, "I reckon I got to light out for the Territory ahead of the rest, because Aunt Sally she's going to adopt me and sivilize [sic] me, and I can't stand it."[15]

Many young people who read *On the Road* found themselves looking for the same thing. It was the life of the hip, Beat Generation of Americans who had walked away from a middle-class lifestyle. They were searching for something freer and trying to enjoy life in the moment. Their hero was Jack Kerouac.

The Pitfalls of Fame

There is an old saying that goes, "Be careful, you might get what you wish for." Jack Kerouac had hoped to become a famous writer. In 1957, he achieved his goal. Kerouac went on television, but he admitted to being "plenty scared."[16] More interviews followed, and book parties were given by his publisher to promote his new book. At one party, held in Kerouac's honor, he never appeared. He was too shy to talk with so many people.

Nevertheless, the requests for interviews did not stop. Kerouac agreed to some of the interviews, but he did not feel comfortable being questioned in front of large audiences. Often he drank heavily and took drugs before making an appearance. In 1958, he appeared on a television interview with Mike Wallace (who later achieved fame as a host of the news program, *Sixty Minutes*.) During the interview, Wallace said to Kerouac,

The Lost Generation

Literary critics have compared the Beat Generation to an earlier group of writers and artists. They were called the Lost Generation. Like the Beats, who were trying to forget World War II, the Lost Generation was trying to put World War I behind them. Thousands of Americans had lost their lives in World War I. The Lost Generation writers believed that the war had shown the hollowness of traditional American values. Among these writers were Ernest Hemingway and F. Scott Fitzgerald. In *The Sun Also Rises*, Hemingway showed the senselessness of war and patriotism. In his novel *The Great Gatsby*, Fitzgerald showed the emptiness of material wealth. Writers like Fitzgerald and Hemingway felt that they were stifled by American society. So they left the United States to live in Europe.

Many of these writers made their homes in Paris. Here, they found a more varied society, much like the one that Kerouac was seeking. This society did not include only white Americans but people from many cultures. Many young Americans enjoyed the novels written by Fitzgerald and other writers like him. They were looking for alternatives to what they believed was a very conservative society. During the 1920s, young people danced to the music of the jazz age. Fitzgerald's novels featured many characters that looked for excitement in fast music, alcohol, and love affairs. These people were similar to the Beats of the 1950s. Indeed, as Bruce Cook wrote: the Beats "seemed to identify very closely with the Lost Generation of the 1920s." *The New York Times* compared *On the Road* to *The Sun Also Rises*. *The Times* "predicted that just as *The Sun Also Rises* was the testament of the Lost Generation, *On the Road* would come to be accepted as that [the testament] of the Beat Generation."[17] This prediction proved to be correct.

"You don't sound happy." Kerouac answered, "Oh, I'm tremendously sad, I'm in great despair." "Why?" Wallace asked. To which Kerouac answered, "Oh, it's a great burden to be alive."[18]

Many Americans were critical of the Beats. Author Bruce Cook pointed out that the Beats were regarded as a "threat." He added that

> they questioned the conservative, corporate, and suburban values that were then so widely and publicly extolled [praised]. The Beats not only questioned, they challenged them, and were soon widely publicized as rebels against the system . . . [one that] attracted thousands—tens of thousands— of young people in a very short time.[19]

Many critics looked down on the work of the Beats. They believed that writers like Ginsberg and Kerouac had "little intrinsic worth," according to Cook.[20] Instead of calling writers like Kerouac *Beats*, some critics began referring to them as *beatniks*. This was meant to be a humorous term that poked fun at the *Beats*. The new term combined *Beat* with part of the word *Sputnik*. This was a new satellite that the Soviet Union [now called Russia] had sent up into space. Beatniks seemed to be people whose feet were not planted securely on the ground. To critics, they were from outer space.

Kerouac continued doing interviews, although he did not like them. At the same time his use of drugs and alcohol increased. It was his way of dealing with all the publicity. However, Kerouac's fame led to requests from publishers to publish some of his other work. Articles that were excerpts from his other novels began to appear in magazines such as *Esquire*. Publishers also wanted to acquire entire novels.

Grove Press, one of these publishers, decided to put out *The Subterraneans*. However, the editor at Grove Press, Donald Allen, decided to make substantial changes in Kerouac's writing style. Commas and periods were added to punctuate and shorten the sentences. Kerouac became very upset with these editorial changes. He insisted that his original writing style must be restored before he would allow the novel to be published.

Kerouac continued doing interviews, although he did not like them.

As he wrote Allen:

> Don, I cant possibly go on as a responsible prose artist and also as a believer in the impulses of my own heart and in the beauty of pure spontaneous language if I let editors take my sentences, which are my phrases that I separate by dashes when "I draw a breath," each of which pours out to the tune of the whole story its own rhythmic yawp of expostulation, & riddle them with commas, cut them in half, in threes, in fours, ruining the swing, making what was reasonably wordy prose even more wordy and unnaturally awkward. . . .[21]

When Grove Press finally agreed, Kerouac restored the manuscript to its original form. "I've just finished five exhausting nights correcting the galleys [drafts] of THE SUBTERRANEANS," he wrote Don Allen late in 1957, "restoring the original freeflowing prose according to the original manuscript which I had here, with the exception of a few deft touches you'd made that were in excellent and wise taste."[22]

The Subterraneans was published in 1958. However, the reviews were generally very negative. One critic, David Dempsey in The New York Times, wrote that the story "seeps out here, like sludge from a leaky drain pipe." Critics did not like Kerouac's style of stream-of-consciousness writing in the novel. Nevertheless, that same year, Kerouac's literary agent, Sterling Lord succeeded in selling The Subterraneans to a film studio for fifteen thousand dollars.[23]

> **One critic, David Dempsey in *The New York Times*, wrote that the story "seeps out here, like sludge from a leaky drain pipe."**

With this money, Kerouac could afford the rent on a new home for Memere and himself in Northport, Long Island. Kerouac never learned how to drive a car. Therefore, he asked an old girlfriend, Joyce Glassman, to drive him out to Long Island to look for houses. Kerouac bought a house in Northport that was next to the local high school. His mother moved there from Florida in spring, 1958.

Writing the *Dharma Bums*

At Northport, Kerouac was working on a new novel. It reflected his interest in Buddhism. He called this novel *The Dharma Bums*. The novel is written in a more conventional prose style. The sentences are short, punctuated with commas, and the story moves along chronologically. Kerouac's editor, Malcolm Cowley, suggested that he follow up the success of *On the Road* with a more conventional type of novel like *The Dharma Bums*.

The hero of the Kerouac's new novel was Japhy Ryder. He was based on the poet Gary Snyder. Snyder was one of the West Coast poets who helped launch the Beat movement. He was also a devout follower of Buddhism. Snyder lived simply and often hiked through the countryside. All he carried was a backpack, containing his clothing—Snyder's only possessions. According to Kerouac, Snyder was a true dharma bum. As Kerouac wrote to Snyder, the novel "is mostly about you. . . ."[24] The story was told by a narrator named Ray Smith, who is based on Kerouac himself.

Jack Kerouac began making notes for the novel while he was in North Africa. Then he wrote the novel rapidly. Kerouac typed it in ten long sittings on a piece of continuous scroll paper. He had created the first draft of *On the Road* the same way. After finishing the manuscript, it was submitted to Viking Publishers. A junior editor there made a number of changes in the work that displeased Kerouac. Therefore, he asked Viking to restore the novel to its original form. Viking granted his request and published the novel in October 1958.

At the beginning of the novel, the narrator announced

Kerouac and Buddhism

Jack Kerouac had begun developing an interest in Buddhism during the early 1950s. It seemed to offer him a new approach to making sense of the society in which he found himself. Buddhism was founded during the sixth century B.C. by Siddhartha Gautama, known as the Buddha. Among its principles is dharma, which means religious truth.

In Buddhism there are Four Noble Truths. The first is that life is suffering. According to the Second Noble Truth, the cause of suffering is attachment to earthly desires. These include a desire to be rich or to enjoy physical pleasure. According to the Third Noble Truth, these desires can be overcome. An individual can reach Nirvana, that is, peace and happiness. The way to achieve Nirvana is to follow the Fourth Noble Truth. This is the Eightfold Path.

The Path includes speaking kindly about other people, doing no harm to others, and abstaining from drugs, alcohol and sexual activity for pleasure. This approach appealed to Jack Kerouac, who believed that life was filled with suffering. At one point, he even abstained from alcohol and sexual activity in order to follow the Eightfold Path of Buddhism. Kerouac also practiced meditation. This enables Buddhists to find an inner sense of calm and discover the best ways to walk the Eightfold Path.

that he "was a perfect Dharma Bum myself and considered myself a religious wanderer."[25] Ray Smith hitchhiked across the American countryside. But Ray had not begun to study Buddhism until his meeting with Japhy Ryder. Kerouac describes Ryder as "a kid from eastern Oregon brought up in a log cabin deep in the woods with his father and mother and sister, from the beginning a woods boy, an axman, farmer, interested in animals and Indian lore. . . ."[26] Like Kerouac's meeting with Gary Snyder, the narrator met Japhy, who was a poet. Japhy had also worked as a fire lookout while attending college.

Later in the novel, Kerouac described the trips that Japhy and the narrator took into the mountains. There, they meditated together. During their trip, the narrator described one of Japhy's most important characteristics—"his tremendous and tender sense of charity. He was always giving things, always practicing what the Buddhists call . . . the perfection of charity."[27] Although the narrator, like Kerouac, began to practice many aspects of Buddhism, he did not lose his Catholicism. As critic Matt Theado wrote: "Christianity combines with Buddhism to produce the distinctive Kerouac religious flavor." Although the narrator claimed to have become "a new man" under the influence of Japhy and Buddhism, "he is not a new man; he is the same man made over. He still holds within himself his traditional notions of Catholicism."[28]

Nevertheless, Japhy helped the narrator to see that

there was an alternative to the middle-class lifestyle. As he put it,

> . . . see the whole thing is a world full of rucksack [backpack] wanders, Dharma Bums refusing to subscribe to the general demand that they consume production and therefore have to work for the privilege of consuming, all that crap they didn't really want anyway such as refrigerators, TV sets, cars . . . deodorants and general junk you finally always see a week later in the garbage anyway, all of them imprisoned in a system of work, produce, consume, work, produce, consume, I see a vision of a great rucksack revolution thousands or even millions of young Americans wandering around with rucksacks, going up to the mountains to pray. . . .[29]

". . . I see a vision of a great rucksack revolution thousands or even millions of young Americans wandering around with rucksacks . . ."

After spending some time in the mountains, the narrator went to San Francisco to visit friends. Then he left Japhy and headed eastward. The narrator traveled to Rocky Mount, North Carolina, to see his mother, sister, and brother-in-law. Kerouac had often done the same thing. During his visit, the narrator described a vision that he experienced. Through this vision, he saw that his mother was coughing in bed. The narrator woke up and realized that by applying some medicine to her neck, it would cure the cough. The next day, the cough was gone. Kerouac, himself, had a similar experience while visiting his mother.

Dharma Bums reflected Kerouac's interest in Zen Buddhism.

The narrator remained only a short time in North Carolina before hitting the road. Like Kerouac, he journeyed to Mexico, and then headed west to rejoin Japhy. After spending some time together, Japhy left for the Far East. Snyder himself had gone to Japan, a center of Buddhism, to learn more about the religion. Meanwhile, the narrator took a job as a fire spotter in the Cascade Mountains. Here, he continued to meditate and practice the other principles of Buddhism. At the end of his summer job, the narrator returned to civilization. His religious beliefs have grown even stronger. As the book concludes, he says, "God, I love you . . . I have fallen in love with you, God. Take care of us all, one way or the other."[30]

> **". . . it has a frightening intensity that makes me wonder if they simply don't want somebody to crucify or tear apart limb from limb . . ."**

Success Slips Away

Gary Snyder read the manuscript for *The Dharma Bums* and told Kerouac that he had enjoyed it.[31] Kerouac's notoriety as a spokesman for the Beat Generation continued. He was asked for more interviews, but generally turned them down. Nevertheless he could not hide from some of his adoring fans:

> . . . two girls and two boys came stealing up to sit with me and ask about Beat. It ended up with a screaming drunken midnight supper my mother

setting out a whole roast beef which was all
devoured. . . .[32]

A short time later, Kerouac appeared at a public
discussion on the topic "Is There a Beat Generation?"
It was held at Hunter College in New York. Kerouac
became upset during the discussion and was later
criticized for being drunk.[33]

Shortly after Kerouac's appearance at Hunter
College, *Dharma Bums* was published. But the critics
were not impressed with Kerouac's new novel. Nor
did many readers buy the book. Nevertheless, Kerouac
was forced to attend parties put on by the publisher to
promote his new novel. As he wrote his agent Sterling
Lord, "the only way I can be saved from the fury of New
York and get some time to re organize [sic] my heart and
mind and go on writing," is to leave for Florida.[34]

Because his books were not selling well, Kerouac's
financial situation had begun to decline. Meanwhile,
his agent, Lord, was trying to find a publisher for
some of his other books. Finally Grove Press decided
to publish *Dr. Sax*. The novel was another part of the
Duluoz legend. It was released in 1959. *Maggie Cassidy*
was published in the same year. But neither book
was very successful. One critic described Dr. Sax as
"unorganized" and criticized it for its "unreadability."[35]
Kerouac received an advance of seventy-five hundred
dollars for Maggie Cassidy. This helped him financially,
but the book sold very few copies. A similar fate

occurred to *Mexico City Blues*, which was published about the same time.

The negative publicity about his books made Kerouac feel increasingly depressed. He drank more heavily but still continued writing. During 1959, Kerouac continued selling articles to magazines. These included "The Roaming Beatniks," written with Allen Ginsberg and other members of the Beat poets. At the end of 1959, Kerouac also sold another novel for publication. This was called *Tristessa*. Avon Books purchased the novel for seventy-five hundred dollars. *Tristessa* had been written in 1955 while Kerouac was in Mexico. The heroine, Tristessa, was the name Kerouac gave to a woman he met in Mexico City. She was Esperanza Villeneuva, a drug addict. The book described her life among a group of Mexican drug addicts. Although suffering from addiction herself, Tristessa was a devout Catholic who never lost her faith. In addition, she seemed to exemplify the simplicity and charity of Buddhism, although she was unfamiliar with its principles. The narrator for this book was Jack Duluoz. *Tristessa* is another part of the Duluoz legend.

Unfortunately, *Tristessa* did not help improve Kerouac's standing as a writer. Meanwhile, *Life* magazine, read by millions of Americans, had published a critical article on the Beats. It was called "Beats: Sad But Noisy Rebels." Kerouac was labeled

Kerouac was labeled "Beatdoms Grand Old Man."

Jack Kerouac used his experiences in Mexico City as inspiration for his writing.

"Beatdoms Grand Old Man," and a writer "hatched by the athletic department at Columbia University."[36] Once again, Jack felt that his skills were being unfairly criticized. And it hurt him. As he wrote his friend Gary Snyder: "I'm sick, I'm drunk."[37] He believed that the critics did not appreciate his works or understand the messages in his novels.

Chapter 8

Kerouac's Long Decline

Living in Northport, Long Island, Jack Kerouac found himself the object of publicity seekers during 1960. Young college students wanted to spend time with the leader of the beatniks. This distracted Kerouac from his work. Meanwhile, he had been trying to write a new book, called *Beat Traveler*. This was a series of his travel experiences. As Kerouac tried to write, however, he suffered writer's block. That is, he was unable to put very much on paper. Gradually, he broke through the block and wrote part of the book, which would eventually be called *Lonesome Traveler*. Nevertheless, Kerouac wanted to leave Northport. He hoped to find some quiet spot where he could write without any distractions.

In 1960, he received an offer from a friend, poet Lawrence Ferlinghetti. He recognized Kerouac's problems trying to write with so many distractions. Ferlinghetti offered his cabin to Kerouac so he could spend some time alone. The cabin was located in Big Sur, a beautiful coastal area in California south of San Francisco. As Kerouac wrote Ferlinghetti:

> I'll be out there in time for July 22. . . . I'm at the end of my nerves. . . . What I need now is a rest, is sleeping in my bag under the stars again, is quiet meditative cookings of supper, reading by oil lamp, singing, sitting by beach with note book and occasional wine—But seriously the other night I knew I was headed for a genuine, my first real mental breakdown if I didn't get away from everybody for at least 2 months. . . .[1]

What was supposed to be a relaxing retreat for Kerouac turned into a nightmare. Alone, Kerouac reflected on his own recent failures as a writer. He also thought about his own death. Partway through his stay at Big Sur, Kerouac suffered a nervous breakdown. Finally he decided to escape the loneliness of Big Sur for San Francisco.

Once in San Francisco, Kerouac stayed with Ferlinghetti, where he eventually recovered. He visited Neal and Carolyn Cassady. Neal Cassady had recently been released from two years in prison for possession of marijuana. While staying at the Cassadys, Kerouac told Carolyn about his problems dealing with writer's block and handling his fame as a novelist. He also began a love affair with a woman named Jacky Gibson. She was a friend of Neal Cassady's. Indeed Cassady and Gibson had previously been involved in an intimate relationship. At one point, Kerouac and Gibson planned to get married. But as biographer Gerald Nicosia wrote:

As their marriage plans became more concrete Jack grew more frightened. . . . [H]e began doing everything in his power to convince Jacky that marriage to him would be disastrous. He told her that he couldn't be a father to Eric [Gibson's son], and that, besides, his own mother would be unbearably lonely without him.[2]

Later in 1960, Kerouac returned to New York, without Gibson. He was simply unable to carry on a long-term intimate relationship with a woman. The only woman to whom he remained closely attached was his mother.

Lonesome Traveler

In December 1960, Kerouac's book *Lonesome Traveler* was published. It included stories about his trips to California. There were also stories about his service aboard the U.S.S. *William Carruthers* in World War II, his travels in Europe, as well as his job as a fire watcher. As one reviewer put it, ". . . it has flashes of poetry, truth, daffiness, lapses of embarrassing writing, and in the end it is much more readable than most 183-page books I could think of."[3] Another reviewer said, "Quite obviously any 9 to 5'er in America would . . . do what Kerouac has done, if he had sufficient courage. . . ."[4] These reviews helped revive Kerouac's spirits and gave him more confidence as a writer.

"Quite obviously any 9 to 5'er in America would . . . do what Kerouac has done, if he had sufficient courage."

Lawrence Ferlinghetti

Lawrence Ferlinghetti was born in New York in 1919. However, he was raised during his early childhood in France. French became his first language. In the 1920s, Ferlinghetti returned to the United States, learned to speak English, and even became a Boy Scout. Ferlinghetti attended the University of North Carolina and after graduation joined the United States Navy. He served during World War II, rising to the rank of lieutenant commander. After the war, he received a master's degree from Columbia University and a doctorate from the Sorbonne, a university in Paris.

In 1953, Ferlinghetti founded the City Lights Bookstore in San Francisco. He also started the City Lights publishing company, which published many of the works written by the Beats. The Beat poets and novelists read many of their works at his bookstore. Among these, was *Howl*, by Allen Ginsberg, which was published by City Lights. Ferlinghetti became a well-known painter and poet. In 1958, he published a book of poems called *A Coney Island of the Mind*. It has become a best seller. Ferlinghetti's work has been honored by many prizes, and in 1998 he became the poet laureate of San Francisco.

Once he was back in New York, however, Kerouac became involved in a legal battle with his former wife, Joan. She wanted him to pay for some of the financial costs of raising the girl she claimed was their daughter, Janet. Joan Haverty was interviewed for a magazine article where she accused Kerouac of earning lots of money and not sharing it with her or their daughter. This hurt Kerouac's feelings. He was making very little money from the sale of his books. In addition, Kerouac claimed that Janet was not his child. However, he finally agreed to work out a compromise in court to pay Haverty fifty-two dollars a month in child support.

During the legal battle with his former wife, Kerouac met his daughter for the first time. Janet accompanied her mother and father to lunch at a bar in Brooklyn, New York. Nevertheless, Kerouac did not forgive Haverty for forcing him to pay child support. He told his friends that Joan was lying and that Janet was not really his daughter.[5]

Big Sur

Meanwhile, Kerouac had completed a new novel, *Big Sur*. In only ten nights during fall 1961, he wrote the novel on a roll of paper in his typewriter. Kerouac had used a similar approach in writing *On the Road*. While writing the novel, Jack was taking large amounts of the dangerous stimulant, Benzedrine.

The novel *Big Sur* reintroduced readers to Jack Duluoz. In this novel, Kerouac returned to his stream of consciousness style of writing. In one passage, he wrote about his decision to travel to Big Sur.

> It's the first trip I've taken away from home (my
> mother's house) since the publication of "Road"
> the book that "made me famous" and in fact so
> much so I've been driven mad for three years
> by endless telegrams, phonecalls, requests, mail,
> visitors, reporters, snoopers (a big voice saying
> in my basement window as I prepare to write a
> story:—ARE YOU BUSY?) or the time the reporter
> ran upstairs to my bedroom as I sat there in my
> pajamas trying to write down a dream—Teenagers
> jumping the six-foot fence I'd had built around my
> yard for privacy—Parties with bottles yelling at
> my study window "Come on out and get drunk,
> all work and no play makes Jack a dull boy!"[6]

In *Big Sur*, Jack Duluoz, went by train to California. At first he seemed to enjoy the beauty of the pacific coast. But after a few days, he said, "I began to get bored. . . ."[7] Gradually, boredom turned to "an awful realization that I have been fooling myself all my life thinking there was a next thing to do to keep the show going and actually I'm just a sick clown and so is everybody else. . . ."[8] Duluoz decided to leave Big Sur and traveled to San Francisco. There he visited Lorenzo Monsanto, a character based on Lawrence Ferlinghetti. He also saw Cody Pomeray, a character based on Neal Cassady. Jack had written about Pomeray in *Visions of Cody*. During Duluoz's stay in San Francisco, there was a lot of heavy drinking. Duluoz also began a love affair with a woman, called Billie in the novel, who was based on Jacky Gibson.

None of these activities, however, seemed to help Kerouac feel any happier. Duluoz eventually returned to Big Sur, where he suffered a nervous breakdown. During this breakdown, Duluoz realized that his Buddhist beliefs could not save him. Instead, he turned back to Catholicism. As Duluoz struggled with the devil, he said that the "angels are laughing and having a big barn dance in the rocks of the sea, nobody cares any more—Suddenly as clear as anything I ever saw in my life, I see the Cross."[9] Finally, after a terrible night at Big Sur, his madness ended. Duluoz could once again return to writing.

Big Sur was published in September 1962, but the reviews were not very positive. Both *Big Sur* and *Visions of Gerard* had been purchased by Robert Giroux for ten thousand dollars. This was a large amount of money, but Giroux still had confidence in Kerouac's ability as a writer. However, one reviewer called *Big Sur* something written by "a perpetual adolescent." Another reviewer called Jack's work a "flood of trivia."[10]

Ferlinghetti believed that Kerouac was being treated unfairly by the critics. He wrote a letter to *Time* magazine that had printed a critical review of Kerouac's new work. Ferlinghetti's letter began: "Your snide, sneering, condescending, semi-literate, semi-dishonest, spiteful attack on Jack Kerouac and his latest book, BIG SUR, is disgusting." But *Time* never printed the letter.[11]

To escape the critical reviews, Kerouac traveled north to New England where he visited with an old friend, John Clellon Holmes. At Holmes's house in Connecticut, Kerouac spent much of the time drinking. Soon he left Connecticut and went north to his boyhood home, Lowell.

Kerouac visited the family of his old friend Sebastian (Sammy) Sampas. Kerouac had maintained a correspondence with Sampas's sister Stella. According to Kerouac's biographer Gerald Nicosia, Stella had "loved him since he first came to her house to visit Sammy."[12] This occurred during the 1930s, when Kerouac was still a boy. Kerouac spent much of his time with Stella's brother Tony. They often went drinking at a bar owned by Tony's brother, Nick. It was called the Old 66 Café.

> **Kerouac spent much of the time drinking.**

Kerouac left Lowell late in 1962. His mother was living in Orlando, Florida, to be with Nin. But Kerouac did not like the hot, humid weather in Orlando. Instead of going back there, Kerouac told his mother that he preferred to live in Northport. It was near the excitement of New York City. Late in December, Kerouac and his mother moved back to Northport.

In Northport, Kerouac began working on a novel, called *Vanity of Duluoz*. While he worked on this book, another novel that Kerouac had written was published early in 1963. *Visions of Gerard* described Kerouac's relationship with his brother, Gerard. Kerouac had actually written this book in 1956. Once again, the critics wrote negative reviews about Kerouac's work. As one reviewer said, "in someone else's hands, it could have been moving."[13] Kerouac was stung by the negative reviews. He wrote his friend, John Clellon Holmes: "I'm filled with that sickened feeling that comes after the reviewers have done with one's latest book."[14]

Kerouac's heavy drinking continued during 1963 and 1964. Finally, his mother decided that the only way to cut down his drinking was to move him away from New York City. She believed that he had too many friends there to go drinking with him.

Final Novels

Late in 1964, Kerouac and his mother returned to Florida. This time they lived in St. Petersburg. Shortly after their return, however, Kerouac's sister suffered a heart attack and died. Her husband had moved out of the house a few months earlier to live with another woman. After moving, he spoke with Nin on the telephone. Kerouac believed that the telephone call may have upset her so much that she was stricken with a heart attack. Nin died at age forty-five. Kerouac wrote John Clellon Holmes:

> Nin died and as time goes on I think about it more and more, in my own way. . . . Youth has a way of sluffing off death and graves and even makes purple armpit poetry about it, as I did. But when in real life there's a red-neoned funeral parlor on the end of your street, . . . gloom hits you. . . . The trouble here is, Nin woulda had a lot of fun with me and

117

my Maw here, picnics etc. a very stimulating city
is St. Petersburg, you'd be surprised.[15]

After recovering from the shock of Nin's death,
Kerouac continued working on *Vanity of Duluoz*. In
this book, he described his life from the late 1930s to
the early 1940s. This period included his adolescence
in Lowell as well as his student days at Columbia
University.

Early in 1965, Kerouac left Florida for a brief trip
to Paris, France. He hoped to do some research on the
Kerouac family. Kerouac wanted to find out more about
his family's origins in Brittany on the Atlantic coast. He
spent much of the time in Paris drinking, and found out
very little about his family. Nevertheless, his experiences
became the basis of another book. This was written after
his return from France. Called *Satori in Paris*, it was sold
to Grove Press for an advance of two thousand dollars.[16]
Kerouac wrote the book in seven nights, while drinking
heavily. After completing the book, he went out drinking
with a group of college students for five days.[17]

Satori in Paris was published in 1966. Meanwhile,
Kerouac had decided that he did not want to continue
living in Florida. The weather was too hot for him, and
his sister was no longer there. Kerouac decided on a
cooler climate on Cape Cod, Massachusetts—not too far
from his hometown in Lowell. But he found that as soon
as people knew a famous writer was there, they began
to annoy him.

However, a much larger problem than his fame

suddenly confronted him. In September, Kerouac's mother suffered a massive stroke. After several weeks in the hospital, she came home. Both Kerouac and his mother loved cats, so he bought her two kittens to keep her company.[18]

Although Kerouac loved his mother, he realized that he could not care for her alone. In the meantime, his relationship with Stella Sampas had grown much closer. In 1964, during one of his visits to Lowell, they had even discussed marriage. Kerouac asked Sampas to help him care for his mother after her stroke. She agreed to move down to Cape Cod. Kerouac and Sampas then decided to get married. She wrote Gabrielle Kerouac in 1966:

> **"I love Jack—have loved him very much for a very long time and have never given the thought of marrying anyone but him."**

> As you know, Jack did come to Lowell and again brought up the subject of he and I getting married. . . . This much I can write, I love Jack—have loved him very much for a very long time and have never given the thought of marrying anyone but him. I look at myself in the mirror, and this is what holds me back. I am no beauty. Probably too old to bear children. Jack deserves much more than I can offer. This much I can offer—love—devotion and each and every effort to make him happy.[19]

On November 19, 1966, Kerouac and Sampas were married. Early in 1967, the couple moved to Lowell, along with his mother. There Stella Kerouac could care

Jack Kerouac laughs in a friend's home in Lowell, Massachusetts, in 1967.

for Gabrielle Kerouac as well as her own mother, who was also very sick.

In Lowell, Kerouac continued working on *Vanity of Duluoz*. He also continued visiting bars and drinking heavily. At this point, Kerouac had very little money from the sale of his books. As a result, Stella Kerouac was thinking about getting a job to support them. Without her at home, Gabrielle Kerouac would have had no one to care for her. The burden was more than Jack Kerouac wanted to handle. Therefore, he asked his agent, Sterling Lord, for a loan. Lord gave him a small amount of money until his new novel could be sold to a publisher. Jack finished the novel in May 1967. He celebrated by going out drinking with friends in Lowell. In fact, by this time he was drinking a quart of Scotch whiskey as well as some beer every day.[20]

In 1968, *Vanity of Duluoz* was published. This book's

Comings and Goings

In November 1967, Jack received a visit from his daughter, Janet. She was fifteen years old, pregnant, and on her way to Florida with her boyfriend. It was a short visit, and the last time Jack and Janet saw each other. They had very little to say during the short visit. Early in 1968, Jack was stunned to learn that he would never see his old friend Neal Cassady again. Cassady's body was found in Mexico near a railroad track. He apparently died from an overdose of drugs after a bout of heavy drinking. Jack learned of Cassady's death from Carolyn. By this time, she had divorced her husband.

title came from a passage in the Bible. The passage states that fame, wealth, and material possessions are vanity—that is, pursuing them is a pointless waste of time. According to critic Matt Theado, Kerouac had come to the realizations that "the glories of life in between—on the football field, in war, in literary success—are merely flashes of vanity."[21]

Once again, the critics gave Kerouac's novel poor reviews. As one reviewer wrote: "A publisher with any real faith in the glow that occasionally generates from a page of any of Kerouac's slapdash novels would not have published this book as it stands."[22]

Last Days

Later in 1968, Kerouac, along with his wife and mother, left Lowell for Florida. They moved to St. Petersburg on the same street where Jack had lived earlier. Jack continued to do some writing, but he earned very little money. During 1969, he worked on a new novel, called *Pic*. In this novel, Kerouac described his own experiences as if they had happened to an African-American boy, named Pic. In September, Kerouac visited an African-American bar in St. Petersburg. There, he became involved in a terrible fight, which left him injured and in jail. Stella Kerouac picked him up and brought him home.

There, he became involved in a terrible fight, which left him injured and in jail.

Meanwhile, years of heavy drinking had taken their

Toward the end of Kerouac's life, his health declined as he drank more and more alcohol.

toll on Kerouac. He had developed severe liver problems and internal bleeding. On October 19, Kerouac began coughing up blood. His wife rushed him to the hospital. Although the doctors tried to save him, they were unsuccessful. Kerouac died of liver problems on October 21, 1969. Although his reputation had declined, he was still an important public figure. His death was announced on the CBS Evening News.

Chapter 9

The Legacy of Jack Kerouac

Jack Kerouac was a very talented writer with a complex, troubled personality. He was always an outsider, who was not comfortable in conventional America. Kerouac helped shape the Beat Generation of American poets and writers who rebelled against the standards of American literature. He also became their leading spokesman. The Beats influenced American culture, not only during Kerouac's life, but long after his death.

The Shaping Forces

Much of Kerouac's personality was formed during the 1920s and 1930s when he grew up in the small, working-class city of Lowell, Massachusetts. Lowell had been the leading city of the nineteenth century Industrial Revolution in America. But by Kerouac's day, Lowell had been overtaken by other American cities. Most of the people there were struggling to make ends meet. The Kerouacs were no different. Kerouac's father drifted from job to job, and it was his mother who held the family together. "Jacky's mother wanted so very much for him," said George J. Apostolos, who grew up with Kerouac in Lowell. "'I can never be what she wants. I can't live with her. I'm disappointing her,' he'd say. Kerouac always tried to please his mother. It seemed to eat away at him."[1] The pressure on him grew after the death of his older brother, Gerard, in 1926. His mother had even higher hopes for him, because he had become the Kerouacs' only son. He first fulfilled these hopes by winning a football scholarship to Columbia University in New York City. But soon Kerouac's life as a student was overtaken by his need for rebellion.

Kerouac broke his leg during a football game at Columbia in his freshman year. Since he could not play football, he focused his attention on his lifelong dream of becoming a writer. Eventually, he dropped out of college—disappointing his parents. Kerouac went to work in a series of low-paying jobs and gathered experiences to put in his writing. As Lucien Carr, his close friend from New York, explained:

> Jack wasn't just *interested* in writing. I mean, whatever else Jack was doing, he had to write. It's like you gotta breathe . . . or eat. He was always writing. . . . And he didn't have to do it right away, which was a great virtue that he had. He really had a memory like few men that you meet. Like he used to say—"That's why they call me Memory Babe," which is what they used to call him in Lowell.[2]

Kerouac made notes about everyone he met, and everything he saw or experienced. His burning goal was to become a published writer. Words defined him and helped bring his own experiences to life.

But at the start, Kerouac had no ambition to define a new style of writing. His first book, *The Town and the City*, published in 1950, was written in a conventional style. It sounded much like other stories of growing up in America. Kerouac hoped that his first novel might help him achieve recognition and fame. But he was disappointed. Very few people read it.

Literature and Lifestyle of a Rebel

Meanwhile, Kerouac had been experimenting with a new style of writing. It was this new style and the experiences he wrote about that eventually made him famous. Kerouac poured out language from his typewriter in much the same way that he thought. It was nonstop and unpunctuated—a steady stream of words that continued for page after page. Nothing like it had been seen before. As a result, publishers were reluctant to buy Kerouac's work and publish it.

The subjects Kerouac wrote about also bothered most publishers. During the 1950s, America was recovering from World War II. The United States had suffered more than 1 million casualties during the war. Americans wanted to forget about the past and enjoy the prosperity of the fifties. They wanted good jobs, new homes, and flashy cars.

Kerouac turned his back on all of these things. With

little or no money in his pocket, he hitchhiked across America, with only the clothes on his back. Kerouac met street bums, hung out in bars, listened to jazz, drank, experimented with drugs, and enjoyed sex. As one of his female friends explained, "Jack was incredibly good-looking, really handsome. He had big blue eyes and black, Indian-type hair. He had an openness, a brash quality. He could be very winning and lovable."[3]

This made it easier for Kerouac to talk to people, make friends, and gather experiences for his books.

> "He had an openness, a brash quality. He could be very winning and lovable."

Kerouac enjoyed living on the road. He was a rebel who defined an alternative lifestyle. However, it appealed to only a small number of people. They were considered "failures" by the conventional standards of most Americans. As a result, his novels did not appeal to the majority of American readers. Kerouac felt frustrated and disappointed, but he did not give up on his dream to become an important writer.

Meanwhile, a few editors at major publishing companies recognized that Kerouac and other writers like him were defining a new style of literature. Indeed, Kerouac's own breakthrough was right around the corner.

On the Road

On the Road, published in 1957, became the bible of the Beat Generation. Kerouac, himself, coined the term *Beat*. As Gilbert Millstein, a critic of *The New York Times*, wrote, the Beats were artists, poets, and writers in

> . . . frenzied pursuit of every possible sensory impression. . . . One gets "kicks"; one "digs" everything, whether it be drink, drugs, sexual promiscuity, driving at high speeds or absorbing Zen Buddhism. . . . The "Beat Generation" was born disillusioned; it takes for granted the imminence of war, the barrenness of politics and the hostility of the rest of society. It is not even impressed by . . . material well-being. . . . It does not know what refuge it is seeking, but it is seeking.[4]

The hero of *On the Road* explained that he was only interested in "the mad ones, the ones who are mad to live, mad to talk, mad to be saved, desirous of everything at the same time, the ones who never yawn or say a commonplace thing, but burn, burn, burn like fabulous yellow roman candles." The hero, Sal Paradise, was based on Kerouac himself. His own rebellious lifestyle was presented through Paradise's adventures on the road.

For young people in the 1950s, Kerouac and the other Beats represented an alternative to the lives of the older generation. Many adolescents were rebellious themselves. Kerouac and his friends became their role models. Among the Beats was the poet Gary Snyder. Not only did he write poetry, but Snyder also spent much of his time hiking through the woods with his backpack. Kerouac wrote about Snyder in his novel, *The Dharma Bums*. "I think Jack saw me, in a funny way, as being another [example of the] twentieth-century American of the West . . . of a tradition of working outdoors and fitting in already with his fascination with the hobo, railroad bum, working man. I was another dimension on that."[5] These people appealed to many young Americans who were searching for an alternative lifestyle.

The Perils of Fame

Soon after *On the Road* hit the bookstores, Jack Kerouac became famous. Most people who knew Jack well described him as a shy man. According to Philip Whalen, a friend of Kerouac's in San Francisco, he became the center of interest after the book. But Kerouac was uneasy with it. "He had so much lack of self-confidence that he would turn on that [others' interest] and say, 'Awww—you're crazy, because I'm a failure. I'm a big flop, and so your interest is misplaced.'"[6]

After his success with *On the Road*, Jack was asked to appear on television programs, radio interviews, and at parties to talk about his book. Many of the interviews were not friendly because a majority of Americans did not approve of Kerouac's lifestyle. As one of his girlfriends, Joyce Glassman (now Joyce Johnson), said, the appearances were "heavy, and it went on for months. And he would make these appearances or be interviewed, and the tone of the interviewing would often be extremely hostile. You know, 'You say this about the Beat Generation. They are terribly immoral people. They take drugs. What are you talking about? These people are awful.'"7

While critics dismissed this book and many of his other novels, many young people seemed to adore Kerouac. He became a celebrity, the king of the Beats. Students from college campuses came to his house and disturbed his writing. They even stole some of his notebooks.

Soon Kerouac was getting into fistfights in bars. His image grew worse. His mother tried to protect him. She tried to keep students from visiting him at the home she shared with her son. She looked over the mail that arrived from critics who disliked his work. She even tried to monitor his telephone calls.

> "It killed him that his books were just being ignored . . ."

While Kerouac appreciated what his mother was trying to do, none of it worked. His carousing only increased. The novels published after *On the Road* generally did not achieve great success. One of Jack's friends during the 1960s was David Amran, a composer, and member of the Beats. "It killed him that his books were just being ignored and being tossed off as inconsequential. That whole thing about being the king of the beatniks was such a manufactured label to criticize everyone. . . ."8 Kerouac eventually suffered a nervous breakdown in the early 1960s and died in 1969 at age forty-seven.

Lawrence Ferlinghetti (left) and Allen Ginsberg talk during the dedication of the Jack Kerouac Commemorative in Lowell, Massachusetts, in 1988.

The Kerouac Legacy

Although Kerouac's life was short, his impact was enormous. His own writing influenced many other people in the Beat Generation. As Gary Snyder said, "I think that I owe a lot to Jack in my prose style, actually. And my sense of poetics has been touched by Jack for sure."[9] Poet Allen Ginsberg changed his entire writing style as a result of Kerouac. Ginsberg's poetry became freer, moving away from lines that rhymed, to more spontaneous poetry. This new style enabled Ginsberg to achieve fame for his own work during the 1950s. Kerouac also helped another Beat writer, William S. Burroughs. Both Kerouac and Ginsberg helped Burroughs edit his most famous Beat novel, *Naked Lunch*. The title for the book was Kerouac's creation.

The Beat writers also defined an alternative lifestyle for young people in the 1950s. Their books were widely read and their lives were emulated by many American youth. But the influence did not stop there. During the 1960s, the Beats were replaced by the hippies. They were rebelling against many of the same values that had been criticized by the Beats. The hippies also experimented with drugs and sexual relationships.

As the decade continued, the rebellion became more vocal. The United States had become more deeply involved in the Vietnam War. Thousands of Americans took to the streets to protest the war. Many of them were young people, fearful of being drafted [required to serve] into the armed forces. Some rebelled against the draft, refusing to serve, or leaving the United States to live in Canada.

In 1968, at the height of the protests, Kerouac appeared on television. He was asked about the connection between the Beats and the hippies. "I'm 46 years old and these kids are 18, but it's the same movement. . . . The hippies are good kids, they're better than the beats. See Ginsberg and I . . . we're all in our forties and we started this and the kids took it up."[10]

Many of these protesters had purchased *On the Road*. The novel was published in a paperback edition. Over the next three decades, more than 3 million copies of the book were sold. The book was a huge best seller. Americans looking for an alternative lifestyle only had to pick up *On the Road*. On the new edition were two hippies. The cover said, "the riotous odyssey of two American drop-outs, by the drop-out who started it all [Jack Kerouac]. . . ."[11]

In the late 1990s, a symposium brought together Ginsberg, Amran, and other Beats. They had continued writing, and their works were widely read. Asked why the Beats still mattered, Amran said, "Young people who have a dream of living the creative life need to know that they can do that. I urge you to see past the 'Burger Kingization' of spiritual and artistic truthfulness that's going on today and find that truth for yourselves."[12]

Critic Bruce Cook has drawn a direct connection between the Beat Generation and the current generation of young people. Today's young people are not in awe of authority. They question what they are told, rebel, and don't hesitate to "drop out in disgust" from American culture. As Cook added, "the present generation is caught in the usual . . . relationship to the past . . . it goes back directly to that legion of artists and frustrated artists, novelists and would-be novelists . . . known . . . as the Beat Generation."[13] That generation was defined and led by Jack Kerouac.

Chronology

1922   Jack Kerouac born in Lowell, Massachusetts.

1926   Kerouac's brother, Gerard, dies.

1936   Flood destroys much of Lowell.

1939   Kerouac graduates from high school.

1940   Enters Columbia University.

1942   Joins the merchant marine.

1943   Joins the Navy; discharged.

1944   Edie Parker and Kerouac marry.

1946   Parker and Kerouac divorce.

1948   Kerouac coins term *Beat Generation*.

1950   *The Town and the City* published.
        Kerouac marries Joan Haverty.

1952   Daughter Janet Haverty born.
        Kerouac writes *Visions of Cody*.

1953   Writes *Maggie Cassidy*, *The Subterraneans*.

1955   Writes *Mexico City Blues* and *Tristessa*.
        Allen Ginsberg reads *Howl*.

1957   *On the Road* published.

1958   *The Subterraneans* and *The Dharma Bums* published.

1959   *Dr. Sax* and *Maggie Cassidy* published.

1960   *Tristessa* and *Lonesome Traveler* published.

1962 *Big Sur* published.

1963 *Visions of Gerard* published.

1966 *Satori in Paris* published.

November 19: Marries Stella Sampas.

1968 *Vanity of Duluoz* published.

1969 Jack Kerouac dies.

Chapter Notes

Chapter 1. Fame

1. Bruce Cook, *The Beat Generation* (New York: Charles Scribner's Sons, 1971), pp. 6–7.
2. Paul Maher, Jr., *Kerouac: The Definitive Biography* (Lanham, Md.: Taylor Trade Publishing, 2004), p. 353.

Chapter 2. Early Life in Lowell

1. Lowell National Historical Park, "History Pages," September 28, 2000, <http://www.nps.gov/lowe/loweweb/Lowell%20History/prologue.htm> (May 1, 2006).
2. Paul Maher, Jr., *The Definitive Biography of Kerouac* (Lanham, Md.: Taylor Trade Publishing, 2004), p. 14.
3. Tom Clark, *Jack Kerouac: A Biography* (New York: Paragon House, 1990), p. 9.
4. Jack Kerouac, *Visions of Gerard* (New York: Farrar, Straus, and Company, 1963), p. 31.
5. Ibid., p. 62.
6. Ibid., p. 83.
7. Ibid., p. 123.
8. Maher, Jr., p. 21.
9. Kerouac, p. 88.
10. Maher, Jr., p. 30.
11. Ibid., p. 28.
12. Gerald Nicosia, *Memory Babe: A Critical Biography of Jack Kerouac* (New York: Grove Press, 1983), p. 46.

13. Ibid., p. 40.
14. Barry Gifford and Lawrence Lee, *Jack's Book: An Oral Biography of Jack Kerouac* (New York: St. Martin's Press, 1978), p. 11.
15. Clark, p. 33.
16. Maher, Jr., p. 56.
17. Clark, p. 41.

Chapter 3. A Writer in New York

1. Lucy Conniff and Richard S. Kennedy, "The Autobiographical Outline for Look Homeward, Angel, by Thomas Wolfe," n.d., <http://www.lsu.edu/lsupress/catalog/Spring2004/Books/Conniff_Autobio_Outline.html> (2005).
2. Barry Gifford and Lawrence Lee, *Jack's Book: An Oral Biography of Jack Kerouac* (New York: St. Martin's Press, 1978), p. 25.
3. Paul Maher, Jr., *The Definitive Biography of Kerouac* (Lanham, Md.: Taylor Trade Publishing, 2004), p. 91.
4. Ann Charters, ed., *Jack Kerouac, Selected Letters, 1940–1956* (New York: Viking, 1995), p. 13.
5. Ibid., p. 16.
6. Paul Marion, ed., *Atop an Underwood: Early Stories and Other Writings, Jack Kerouac* (New York, Viking, 1999), p. 118.
7. Ibid., pp. 57, 61–62.
8. Tom Clark, *Jack Kerouac: A Biography* (New York: Paragon House, 1990), p. 52.
9. Maher, Jr., p. 124.
10. Gifford and Lee, p. 212.
11. Maher, Jr., p. 129.
12. Charters, p. 88.

13. Clark, p. 72.
14. John Andrews, "What Bebop Meant to Jazz History," May 22, 1998, <http://www.wsws.org/arts/1998/may1998/bop-m22.shtml> (May 1, 2006).
15. Charters, p. 105.

Chapter 4. First Novel

1. Douglas Brinkley, ed., *Windblown World: The Journals of Jack Kerouac, 1947–1954* (New York: Viking, 2004), p. xvii.
2. Ibid., p. 8.
3. Ibid., p. 15.
4. Matt Theado, *Understanding Jack Kerouac* (Columbia: University of South Carolina Press, 2000), p. 42.
5. Jack Kerouac, *The Town and the City* (New York: Harcourt Brace and Company, 1950), p. 45.
6. Ibid., p. 89.
7. Ibid., p. 96.
8. Ibid., p. 243.
9. Ibid., p. 307.
10. Ibid., p. 359.
11. Theado, p. 43.
12. Barry Gifford and Lawrence Lee, *Jack's Book: An Oral Biography of Jack Kerouac* (New York: St. Martin's Press, 1978), p. 9.
13. Kerouac, p. 471.
14. Ibid., pp. 498–499.
15. Ann Charters, ed., *Jack Kerouac, Selected Letters, 1940–1956* (New York: Viking, 1995), p. 110.
16. Ibid., p. 149.

17. Ibid., p. 172.
18. John Clellon Holmes, "This Is the Beat Generation," *The New York Times Magazine*, November 16, 1952, <http://www.litkicks.com/Texts/ThisIsBeatGen.html> (May 1, 2006).
19. Brinkley, p. xviii.
20. Charters, pp. 185–186.
21. Brinkley, p. 217.
22. Ibid., p. xx.

Chapter 5. No Easy Road to Success

1. Ann Charters, ed., *Jack Kerouac, Selected Letters, 1940–1956* (New York: Viking, 1995), p. 239.
2. Ibid., p. 243.
3. Paul Maher, Jr., *The Definitive Biography of Kerouac* (Lanham, Md.: Taylor Trade Publishing, 2004), p. 225.
4. Charters, p. 250.
5. Ibid., pp. 247–248.
6. Maher, Jr., p. 230.
7. Charters, p. 356.
8. Matt Theado, *Understanding Jack Kerouac* (Columbia: University of South Carolina Press, 2000), p. 77.
9. Jack Kerouac, *Visions of Cody* (New York: McGraw-Hill, 1972), p. 3.
10. Gerald Nicosia, *Memory Babe: A Critical Biography of Jack Kerouac* (New York: Grove Press, 1983), p. 371.
11. Ibid., pp. 371–372.
12. Kerouac, p. 398.
13. Nicosia, p. 382.

14. Ibid., p. 385.

15. Kerouac, p. xi.

16. Tom Clark, *Jack Kerouac: A Biography* (New York: Paragon House, 1990), p. 115.

17. Ibid., p. 109.

18. Maher, Jr., p. 251.

19. Jack Kerouac, *Dr. Sax* (New York: Grove Wiedenfield, 1959), p. 5.

20. Ibid., p. 33.

21. Ibid., p. 238.

22. Ibid., p. 242.

23. Ibid., p. 245.

24. Charters, p. 383.

Chapter 6. Failure, Then Success!

1. Mike Janssen, "The Influence of Jazz on the Beat Generation," n.d., <http://www.fb10.uni-bremen.de/anglistik/kerkhoff/beatgeneration/BG-Essays.htm> (May 1, 2006).

2. Ann Charters, ed., *Jack Kerouac, Selected Letters, 1940–1956* (New York: Viking, 1995), p. 396.

3. Barry Gifford and Lawrence Lee, *Jack's Book: An Oral Biography of Jack Kerouac* (New York: St. Martin's Press, 1978), pp. 169, 175.

4. Matt Theado, *Understanding Jack Kerouac* (Columbia: University of South Carolina Press, 2000), p. 106.

5. Ibid., p. 110.

6. Charters, p. 399.

7. Gerald Nicosia, *Memory Babe: A Critical Biography of Jack Kerouac* (New York: Grove Press, 1983), p. 440.

8. Ibid., p. 442.

9. Theado, p. 111.

10. Jack Kerouac, *The Subterraneans* (New York: Grove Press, 1958), p. 1.

11. Ibid., p. 16.

12. Ibid., p. 18.

13. Ibid., p. 39.

14. Ibid., p. 81.

15. Ibid., p. 111.

16. Nicosia, p. 448.

17. Jack Kerouac, "Essentials of Spontaneous Prose," August 6, 2004, <http://www.writing.upenn.edu/~afilreis/88/kerouac-spontaneous.html> (May 1, 2006).

18. Nicosia, p. 454.

19. Paul Maher, Jr., *The Definitive Biography of Kerouac* (Lanham, Md.: Taylor Trade Publishing, 2004), pp. 290–291.

20. Charters, p. 429.

21. Jack Kerouac, *Mexico City Blues* (New York: Grove Press, 1959), p. 19.

22. Ibid., back cover.

23. Ann Charters, "Allen Ginsberg's Life," n.d., <http://www.english.uiuc.edu/maps/poets/g_l/ginsberg/life.htm> (2005).

24. "Interview with Allen Ginsberg," n.d., <http://www.levity.com/mavericks/gins.htm> (May 1, 2006).

25. Charters, *Jack Kerouac, Selected Letters, 1940–1956*, pp. 563–564.

Chapter 7. The Voice of a New Generation

1. Ann Charters, ed., *Jack Kerouac Selected Letters, 1957–1969* (New York: Viking, 1999), p. 9.

2. Paul Kane, *Naked Lunch*, © 2000–2006, <http://www.sfreader.com/read_review.asp?ID=139> (May 1, 2006).

3. Jack Kerouac, *On The Road* (New York: Penguin Books, 1976), p. 1.

4. Matt Theado, *Understanding Jack Kerouac* (Columbia: University of South Carolina Press, 2000), p. 55.

5. Douglas Brinkley, ed., *Windblown World: The Journals of Jack Kerouac, 1947–1954* (New York: Viking, 2004), p. 223.

6. Theado, pp. 56–57.

7. Kerouac, p. 1.

8. Theado, p. 57.

9. Kerouac, p. 5.

10. Theado, p. 71.

11. Kerouac, p. 249.

12. Ibid., p. 276.

13. Ibid., p. 307.

14. Ibid., back cover.

15. Bruce Cook, *The Beat Generation* (New York: William Morrow, 1971), p. 37.

16. Tom Clark, *Jack Kerouac: A Biography* (New York: Paragon House, 1990), p. 164.

17. Cook., pp. 48, 71.

18. Clark., p. 169.

19. Cook, p. 10.

20. Ibid., p. 17.

21. Charters, p. 15.

22. Ibid., p. 83.

23. Ibid., p. 119.

24. Ibid., p. 24.

25. Jack Kerouac, *The Dharma Bums* (New York: Penguin Books, 1973), p. 5.

26. Ibid., p. 9.

27. Ibid., p. 75.

28. Theado, pp. 154–155.

29. Kerouac, *The Dharma Bums*, p. 97.

30. Ibid., p. 244.

31. Theado, p. 154.

32. Ibid., p. 136.

33. Ibid., p. 162.

34. Ibid., p. 180.

35. Paul Maher, Jr., *The Definitive Biography of Kerouac* (Lanham, Md.: Taylor Trade Publishing, 2004), p. 392.

36. Ibid., p. 229.

37. Ibid., p. 235.

Chapter 8. Kerouac's Long Decline

1. Ann Charters, ed., *Selected Letters of Jack Kerouac, 1957–1969* (New York: Viking, 1999), p. 260.

2. Gerald Nicosia, *Memory Babe: A Critical Biography of Jack Kerouac* (New York: Grove Press, 1983), p. 616.

3. Paul Maher, Jr., *The Definitive Biography of Kerouac* (Lanham, Md.: Taylor Trade Publishing, 2004), p. 409.

4. Charters, p. 275.

5. Ibid., p. 337.

6. Jack Kerouac, *Big Sur* (New York: McGraw-Hill, 1962), p. 4.

7. Ibid., p. 30.

8. Ibid., p. 41.

9. Ibid., p. 204.
10. Nicosia, p. 637.
11. Charters, p. 346.
12. Nicosia, p. 671.
13. Ibid., p. 648.
14. Charters, p. 371.
15. Ibid., p. 383.
16. Maher, Jr., p. 453.
17. Charters, p. 409.
18. Maher, Jr., p. 456.
19. Charters, pp. 422–423.
20. Nicosia, p. 682.
21. Theado, p. 184.
22. Charters, p. 451.

Chapter 9. The Legacy of Jack Kerouac

1. Barry Gifford and Lawrence Lee, *Jack's Book: An Oral Biography of Jack Kerouac* (New York: St. Martin's Press, 1978), p. 9.
2. Ibid., p. 46.
3. Ibid., p. 175.
4. Ibid., p. 239.
5. Ibid., p. 202.
6. Ibid., p. 218.
7. Ibid., p. 241.
8. Ibid., p. 260.
9. Ibid., p. 203.
10. Paul Maher, Jr., *The Definitive Biography of Kerouac* (Lanham, Md.: Taylor Trade Publishing, 2004), p. 469.
11. Ann Charters, ed., *Selected Letters of Jack Kerouac, 1957–1969* (New York: Viking, 1999), p. 417.

12. J. C. Shakespeare, "Ashcan Rantings and Kind King Light of Mind, Why the Beats Still Matter," n.d., <http://www.altx.com/io/beatgeneration. html> (May 1, 2006).

13. Bruce Cook, *The Beat Generation* (New York: William Morrow, 1971), p. 5.

Glossary

advance—Money paid by a publisher to an author when his or her book is accepted. This money is later taken out of the book's royalties when it is published.

Benzedrine—A type of drug that enables users to stay awake for long periods of time.

book tour—Arrangements made by publishers for authors to tour cities and promote their books.

coureur de bois—French Canadian fur trappers.

excerpts—Small parts of a book.

G.I. Bill—Money given to military veterans to pay for college.

Joual—French dialect spoken by French Canadians.

literary agent—A person who works with writers to bring their manuscripts to editors at major publishing companies.

manuscript—Original draft of a book before it is published.

merchant marine—Operates supply transport ships to U.S. armed forces.

peyote—A hallucinogenic drug.

royalties—Refers to money paid to an author for every copy of his or her book that is sold.

stream of consciousness—Style of writing in which sentences run together like a writer's thoughts.

Selected Works by Jack Kerouac

The Town and the City (1950)

On the Road (1957)

The Dharma Bums (1958)

The Subterraneans (1958)

Mexico City Blues (1959)

Maggie Cassidy (1959)

Dr. Sax (1959)

Tristessa (1960)

Lonesome Traveller (1960)

Scripture of the Golden Eternity (1960)

Book of Dreams (1961)

Pull My Daisey (1961)

Big Sur (1962)

Visions of Gerard (1963)

Desolation Angels (1965)

Satori in Paris (1966)

Vanity of Duluoz (1968)

Scattered Poems (1971)

Pic (1971)

Visions of Cody (1972)

Trip Trap (1973)

Heaven and Other Poems (1977)

Pomes All Sizes (1992)

Good Blonde and Others (1993)

Old Angel Midnight (1993)

Some of the Dharma (1997)

Atop an Underwood (1999)

Orpheus Emerged (2000)

Book of Haikus (2003)

Departed Angels—The Lost Paintings (2004)

Further Reading

Books

Brinkley, Douglas, ed. *Windblown World: The Journals of Jack Kerouac, 1947–1954*. New York: Viking, 2004.

Charters, Ann, ed. *Jack Kerouac, Selected Letters, 1940–1956*. New York: Viking, 1995.

———*The Portable Jack Kerouac*. New York: Viking, 1995.

———*Selected Letters of Jack Kerouac, 1957–1969*. New York: Viking, 1999.

Heims, Neil. *Allen Ginsberg*. Philadelphia: Chelsea Books, 2005.

Kallen, Stuart A. *The History of Jazz*. San Diego: Lucent Books, 2003.

Kherdian, David. *Beat Voices: An Anthology of Beat Poetry*. New York: Holt, 1995.

Lawler, William T., ed. *Beat Culture: Lifestyles, Icons, and Impact*. Santa Barbara, Calif.: ABC-CLIO, 2005.

Maher, Jr., Paul. *Kerouac: The Definitive Biography*. Lanham, Md.: Taylor Trade Publishing, 2004.

McKee, Jenn. *Jack Kerouac*. Philadelphia: Chelsea House Publishers, 2004.

Sandison, David. *Jack Kerouac: An Illustrated Biography*. Chicago: Chicago Review Press, 1999.

Theado, Matt. *Understanding Jack Kerouac*. Columbia, S.C.: University of South Carolina Press, 2000.

Wilkinson, Philip. *Buddhism*. DK, 2003.

Zott, Lynn M. *The Beat Generation: A Gale Critical Companion*. Detroit: Gale, 2003.

CDs

The Jack Kerouac Collection. Santa Monica, Calif.: Rhino Records, 1990.

Readings by Jack Kerouac on the Beat Generation. New York: Verve, 1997.

Sampas, Jim, and Lee Ranaldo, producers. *Jack Kerouac Reads* On the Road. Salem, Mass.: Rykodisc, 1999.

Internet Addresses

The American Museum of Beat Art
   <http://www.beatmuseum.org>

Literary Kicks: Beatitude
   <http://www.litkicks.com>

   *Click on "Beats" at top. Scroll all the way down and
   select "View all for this category."*

The Official Jack Kerouac Website
   <http://www.jackkerouac.com>

Index